Rewriting the Hero and the Quest

Tatiana Golban

Rewriting the Hero and the Quest

Myth and Monomyth in *Captain Corelli´s Mandolin* by Louis de Bernières

Bibliographic Information published by the Deutsche Nationalbibliothek
The Deutsche Nationalbibliothek lists this publication in the Deutsche Nationalbibliografie; detailed bibliographic data is available in the internet at http://dnb.d-nb.de.

Cover image:
"Dance" by Dalila Ozbay

ISBN 978-3-631-65459-0 (Print)
E-ISBN 978-3-653-04667-0 (E-Book)
DOI 10.3726/ 978-3-653-04667-0
© Peter Lang GmbH
Internationaler Verlag der Wissenschaften
Frankfurt am Main 2014
All rights reserved.
PL Academic Research is an Imprint of Peter Lang GmbH.

Peter Lang – Frankfurt am Main · Bern · Bruxelles · New York ·
Oxford · Warszawa · Wien

All parts of this publication are protected by copyright. Any utilisation outside the strict limits of the copyright law, without the permission of the publisher, is forbidden and liable to prosecution. This applies in particular to reproductions, translations, microfilming, and storage and processing in electronic retrieval systems.

www.peterlang.com

Contents

Preface 7

Acknowledgements 9

Introduction 11

1. Theoretical Perspectives and Their Applicability in the Approach to Louis de Bernières 13
   1.1 Defining Myth 13
   1.2 Carl Jung 15
   1.3 Joseph Campbell 20
   1.4 Claude Lévi-Strauss 23
   1.5 Roland Barthes 26

2. Practical Argumentation 31
   2.1 Rethinking the Monomyth of the Hero and the Quest as a Critical Concern 31
   2.2 The Paradigm of the Monomyth of the Hero and the Quest in Joseph Campbell's Conception 33
   2.3 Reimagining the Monomyth of the Hero and the Quest in *Captain Corelli's Mandolin* 41
      2.3.1 Mandras 42
      2.3.2 Captain Antonio Corelli 60
      2.3.3 Pelagia 78

Conclusion 113

References and Further Reading 115

Index 119

Preface

Nowadays, myth enjoys an enhanced attention on the part of comparative literature studies, and is re-evaluated according to new gains and experiences in the various areas of literary science. In the wider context of world and comparative literature, the element related to the aesthetic value of myth has penetrated irrevocably into the literary tradition, representing at the same time a literary fact that fulfils the intellectual needs of modern human beings, in spite of the complex new cultural alternatives, by drawing a strong sense of interest from the reading public as well as critics and exegetes.

The main goal of our study is the examination – through the lens of an appropriate comparative methodology – of the artistic means and procedures used by Louis de Bernières in his novel *Captain Corelli's Mandolin* to represent, in literary terms, concerns and characters of the ancient myth and monomyth as literary archetypes in their modern reception. The emphasis is on the manner in which the monomyth of the hero and the quest has been subject to essential thematic changes with the purpose of adapting them to a specific artistic view, which is that of Louis de Bernières as a particular writer, and a specific target audience living in a different – which is postmodern – period and cultural background.

In the studies on the reappearance of myth in literature, it has been affirmed that ancient myths "renew themselves as they are transmitted from one literary version to another" (Kushner, 2001, p. 300), revealing a

> paradox of permanence and transformation. The haunting question that arises for the critic and the historian as well as for the theoretician of literature and those who study the anthropological, psychological, and sociological aspects of imagination is that of the resilience of myths. How is it that these ancient narratives – very often Greek myths in the case of the literatures of the West – survive and revive with ever-renewed meaning for writers, readers, and spectators of subsequent periods? What is the source of their power of resurgence? (Kushner, 2001, p. 300)

The answer, given by the same critic, is that

> the permanence of myths as they manifest themselves in modern literature lies not in fixity of narrative detail, nor in an ontological unity of the human mind as enshrined in the world of myths, nor again in the preservation of a classical flavour, but in the very dynamics of myth itself. (Kushner, 2001, p. 303)

The monomyth of the hero and the quest, like the ethno-religious myth, the literary myth or the literalised myth, reveals permanence, literary continuity, and flexibility as a literary pattern open to innovation and creative originality. The monomyth of the hero and the quest, like other types of myth, is also a well-structured system preserving the pattern of journey of the hero and some essential symbolic situations unaltered regardless of the time and space of action.

At the same time, the monomyth, as a dynamic system of symbols and archetypes, perpetually renews itself. The framework of the monomyth of the hero and the quest provides the opportunity for flexibility by presenting the exterior journey performed by the protagonist as mainly an inner journey with its own symbolical significance of the search for the self and the accomplishment of one's true goal in life. This demonstrates once again the truth of the statement that myth survives and continues its development, and remains representative and initiatory for the individual and community within literary discourse.

The first chapter of our book represents the theoretical and methodological basis of our study, which is in line with the most important and accessible bibliography and contributions by specialists in the field, which are fully accepted internationally, namely those by Carl Jung, Joseph Campbell, Claude Lévi-Strauss, and Roland Barthes.

The second chapter represents the practical side of the research, which includes the approach to the text, where we have used principles of textual interpretation applied in the areas of literary theory and criticism, comparative literature, literary history, intertextuality, archetypal criticism, and thematology. In particular, the book targets those readers who are familiar with goals, methods and styles of myth criticism and archetypal critical discourse, and especially with their current postmodern and postmodernist perspectives.

Although Louis de Bernières is a famous and important contemporary novelist, and his work *Captain Corelli's Mandolin* has been translated and sold all over the world as a best-seller, there are no academic studies – neither books nor articles – that focus methodologically and theoretically on it. We attempt to partially overcome this handicap by our book in which we have focused on various thematic and structural aspects which have been practically ignored so far by this line of criticism. We have also progressed to certain interpretative modalities of analysis of our own and the results of the research could become starting points for a number of other studies in the domain of Comparative Literature and that of English literature.

The book meets the requirements of a teaching aid and regards the needs of the students in their English and Comparative Literature classes, introducing them to the areas of myth and contemporary fiction. Also, the book is useful to experts in literary studies, or to a more general reader whose knowledge of certain aspects of myth and literature might be enriched by the present book.

Acknowledgements

I owe my first acknowledgement to my students at Namik Kemal University in Turkey, whose comments and pertinent remarks helped shape many of my ideas. Above all, I am grateful to my former doctoral supervisor Professor Sergiu Pavlicencu who greatly enlarged my understanding of ancient and modern literary interaction and provided for me a model of approach to myths and archetypes. I am also thankful to my husband, Petru Golban, whose encouragement and well-aimed critical remarks were most helpful. My gratitude is also for my daughters Beatrice and Patricia for their understanding and support during the writing of this book. Finally, I am indebted to my colleagues Hasan Boynukara, Cansu Ozge Ozmen, and Irfan Atalay for their intellectual assistance, scholarly advice, critical comment, and competent suggestions that assisted me in the process of preparation of this book.

Introduction

Louis de Bernières' book *Captain Corelli's Mandolin* (1994) is a work which uses myth, in general, and the monomyth of the hero and the quest, in particular, as a medium to represent human existence in a postmodern world. Through the examination of the mythical restructuring as shaped by de Bernières, emerges the assumption that his work creates a distinctive depiction of reality, characteristic to postmodern literature.

Although the purpose of our study is not the integration of Louis de Bernières' novel into any of the postmodern experimental trends, we should mention that the emphasis of the author upon the transformation of myth, as well as his continuous tendency to deconstruct and then to reconstruct semantically the key components of the mythical models, may be qualified as postmodern. The postmodernity or postmodern period includes both traditional, realistic literature and experimental, innovative literary practice which is referred to as postmodernism, and it is claimed that de Bernières is not a realist but rather postmodernist by approaching reality through myth. He is also an author of magical realism, yet *Captain Corelli's Mandolin* is neither a realistic novel nor a text of magical realism, and, in the case of this work, the British novelist is not a traditional, concerned with reality and socially concerned writer, and not exactly an experimental postmodernist, but definitely postmodern.

In order to avoid the possible entrapment in a mythical situation or into an archetypal pattern, the writer uses a well-known prototype with the aim of rethinking myth and monomyth in an original way, as a result of which the known and predictable situation and archetypal character are changed and come to denote new meanings.

Consequently, in Louis de Bernières' novel, the "protean" characteristic acquired by myth thwarts the recreation of predictable meanings, connotations, and outcomes of an easily recognizable situation, and the mythical situation and the archetypal pattern and character are not merely revived, but renewed and reloaded with new perspectives of thematic and structural significance.

De Bernières does not simply unravel and reconstruct myth and monomyth, but, in a typically postmodern manner, achieves a playful undermining of the conventional, modern Western ideological patterns, constantly engaging the reader into the creation of new ideas and possibly new meanings.

Throughout the course of this study, we attempt to reveal the postmodern representation of myth and the monomyth of the hero and the quest in de Bernières' work. Through the close textual analysis, we attempt to expose the most vivid patterns of his deconstruction and reconstruction of the monomyth, patterns which serve as powerful metaphors that reflect the great communal transformations which mark the passage from the modern to the postmodern.

Louis de Bernières' novel *Captain Corelli's Mandolin* is a work that uses myth and monomyth to convey the deconstruction of the modern ideals. In the postmodern fashion, the writer has revived, rethought, reimagined, and rewritten the monomyth of the hero and the quest, as well as the Biblical myth of salvation, the myth of the golden age, and the utopia myth. At the same time, the atrocities of the Second World War, which are represented in the novel, made the author emphasize and reconstruct the myth of descent into the underworld, as well as the various thematic perspectives of the totalitarian myth, the Dictator myth, and the Apocalypse myth.

The main concern of our study is the monomyth of the hero and the quest, which we also refer to as the hero myth. We focus also on various related aspects, such as history, character, and dominating mentality, among others.

Myth and history are generally considered as opposing modes of explanation. However, in de Bernières' novel, these two concepts do not exclude one another; on the contrary, history is represented as a myth, a fable, and a construction of human imagination. The writer deconstructs the all-encompassing modern ideologies with their mythical models rooted in Christianity and in the legends of Western Civilization, and re-contextualizes them.

Louis de Bernières plays with the conventional meanings of myths, deconstructing their established connotation. At the same time, he confers new meanings which radically modify the "universal truth" of myth, allowing its perpetual change and new interpretations. Deconstruction, playfulness, semiological changes, the concern with myth and history, as well as the alterations of the absolutisms of the modern era, emphasize the novel's postmodern nature.

1. Theoretical Perspectives and Their Applicability in the Approach to Louis de Bernières

1.1 Defining Myth

Since Louis de Bernières' *Captain Corelli's Mandolin* revives and reconstructs the ancient literary myth, in general, and the monomyth of the hero and the quest, in particular, rather than the ethno-religious one, as our starting point, we are aware that it is impossible to embark on a study of "the monomyth of the hero and the quest" without first considering the meaning of the word "myth". Myth, as it is explained in *The Oxford English Dictionary*, gives us a surprisingly short definition. It states that myth is "a purely fictitious narrative usually involving supernatural persons, actions, or events, and embodying some popular idea concerning natural or historical phenomena". It suggests that this word might refer to "a fictitious or imaginary person or object". Traditionally, it is considered that the word "myth" comes from the Greek *mythos*, which means "story". In the course of time, subsidiary meanings appeared in the common usage of the term, such as "an untrue or popular tale, a rumour".

These explanations of the term "myth" being far from satisfactory, we rather focus our attention on mythographers, scholars that should provide us with more helpful understanding and description.

David Leeming, in *The World of Myth*, claims that "human beings have traditionally used stories to describe or explain things they could not otherwise" (Leeming, 1990, p. 3). Looking at myth through this perspective, makes us see myth more than a story of what happened, or a story told for amusement.

Michael Bell stresses the difficulty of defining myth, claiming that "it means both a supremely significant foundational story and a falsehood" (Bell, 1997, p. 1).

Eric Dardell states that myth is a "typical" story with immediate and powerful impact (Dardell, 1984, p. 232), while Riane Eisler claims that it concerns "larger-than-life" persons and events which are transmitted from generation to generation (Eisler, 1997, p. viii).

R. G. Stone calls attention to myth's moral aspect (Stone, 1967, p. 177), whereas John J. White insists upon the continuous recurrence of myth stressing its own resonant force by the paradox of permanence and transformation (White, 1971, p. 25).

One of the most important religious historians, Mircea Eliade, suggests the following definition of myth:

> myth is regarded as a sacred story, and hence a "true history", because it always deals with *realities*. The cosmogonist myth is "true" because the existence of the World is there to prove it; the myth of the origin of death is equally true because man's mortality proves it, and so on. (Eliade, 1963, p. 6)

Consequently, for Eliade, myth is a sacred, timeless and eternal story. Myth recounts a sacred story; it relates an event that took place in primordial times, during the legendary era when things began.

Therefore, while the literary narrative refers to a historical moment, the narrative of myth, according to Eliade, presupposes a temporal form which is reversible and an aspect of sacred time. Also, the literary narrative tends to a dialectical resolution of the conflict, whereas the narrative of myth offers initiation within an altered situation; and the literary narrative represents a relative form of truth, but the narrative of myth, Eliade argues, discloses eternal and absolute truths, which are fundamental stories.

Other scholars see myth from a totally different perspective: for Sigmund Freud, myth is the projection of psychology onto the external world (Freud, 1953–1966, p. 258), whereas Jean-François Lyotard perceives it as a form of fantasy (Lyotard, 1989, p. 72).

Gilbert Durand, in his *Les Structures Antropologiques de l'Imaginaire* (1960), suggests that myth is "a dynamic system of symbols, archetypes and schemas, a dynamic system that tends, when prompted by a schema, to take the form of a story"; consequently, the source of the power of the resurgence of myths lies in its own "dynamics" (Durand cited in Brunel, 1992, p. x).

Andre Jolles in *Formes Simples* proposes to view myth as "the place where an object is created from a question and its answer (…), myth is the place where, starting from its innermost nature, an object becomes creation" (Jolles cited in Brunel, 1992, p. xi).

For Thomas Stearns Eliot and Northrop Frye, literature is a universal order, a complete world where all the topics, characters and stories we find in literature belong to a vast totality whose principle of integration, according to Claudio Guillen, is explained by "the persistence of ancient myths":

> Understand by myth not only a collective fantasy that incarnates ideals and memories (…) but an effort of the imagination to unite the world (…). Literature and myth do not describe or measure the surroundings in which we live but absorb them and shape them, converting them into our space, more human, more intimate, and also more bearable. (Guillen, 1993, p. 238)

In accordance with the important contribution made by Olga Freidenberg (whose ideas are close to those of Claude Lévi-Strauss and the members of the Tartu semiotic school) in the area of structural and semiotic analysis of myth and literature, the emergence of literature in general is to be sought in the transition from the mentality based on mythical and mythological images to a thought based on formal-logical concepts, that is, the transition from mythical to conceptual thought. The content of mythic images is inherited, thus becoming the texture of some new concepts (Freidenberg, 1997).

In other words, the creative perception of the writer means in reality *changing* the primary scheme of myth, transforming it "through losses, through mythemes originating in other myths, etc." (Durand, 1998, p. 303) and "creating" an original symbolic situation as a new literary and mythological tradition, next to the diversity of angles relating to the topic, theme, representation of characters, typology of the archetype, the fundamental situation, and strategies for the structural organization of the text.

The topic, theme, fundamental situation, and archetype represent the content of a mytheme, "the smallest unit of discourse bearing mythical significance", situated "at the core of the myth", being of a "structural nature" ("archetypal nature" in the Jungian sense), or "schematic" nature by Gilbert Durand, where "the verbal dynamic dominates the substantiality" and which can be used by authors from different periods affected by and "depending on repression, censorship, morals or ideologies of a certain period and certain milieu" (Durand, 1998, pp. 303–304).

1.2 Carl Jung

The work of Carl Jung, which underpins so much the contemporary thinking about myth, deserves our special consideration, since Louis de Bernières' novel has been greatly influenced by Jung's theories. The key to Jungian theory of myth lies in his idea of a universal collective unconscious, "the repository of man's experience" which is comprised of "archetypes" (Jung, 1969).

According to Jung, archetypes are some emblematic forms of behaviour which manifest themselves as ideas and images to the conscious mind. As he explains,

> the archetypes, which are pre-existent to consciousness (…) appear in the part they actually play in reality: as a priori structural forms of the stuff of consciousness. They do not in any sense represent things as they are in themselves, but rather the forms in which things can be perceived and conceived. Naturally, it is not merely the archetypes that govern the particular nature of perceptions. They account only for

the collective components of a perception. As an attribute of instinct they partake of its dynamic nature, and consequently possess a specific energy which causes or compels definite modes of behaviour or impulses; that is, they may under certain circumstances have a possessive or obsessive force (numinosity!). (Jung, 1963, p. 347)

In Carl Jung's opinion, archetypes produce and form all our most powerful thinking, initiating science, philosophy, mythology, and religion. Being influenced by Arthur Schopenhauer's writings, Jung introduces the idea of the ultimate unity of existence, which, in his opinion, is situated outside space and time. Archetypes find their origin in this transcendental unity, and although they might be formed by consciousness into opposing concepts, they continue to be the facets of the same reality. Jung believes that the continuing influence of archetypes clarifies the reoccurrence of the identical motifs throughout world mythology, which appear in the thoughts and dreams of people unaware of mythical tradition.

In case we approve of Jungian theory, then it may well provide an explanation of myth's continuous reoccurrence and influence, when the motifs it employs are generated by our most basic motivating instincts. For Jung, archetypes represent "deposits of the constantly repeated experiences of humanity"; therefore, there are chances that if our experiences change, so will do the archetypes that instigate our myths (Jung, 1983, p. 68).

Jung also insists upon the organizing function of archetypes, given that they "behave empirically like agents that tend towards the repetition of these same experiences" (Jung, 1983, p. 71).

In Jung's own mythic pattern, he considers four major archetypes which transmit us the story, as it were, of the psyche. Jung insists that although collective, these archetypes must be realized on an individual level. First, he considers the "ego", the conscious mind; this represents the human being's sense of purpose and identity. Second is the "shadow", or the unconscious aspect of the human psyche, which ego attempts to annihilate or disregard, frequently represented in dreams by a person of the same gender as the ego. The ego should first confront and then assimilate the power of the shadow. Third, Jung considers the "anima" (Latin, "soul"), the unconscious, feminine element of a male personality; and the "animus" (Latin, "spirit"), the unconscious, masculine element of a woman's personality. In other words, the former is the man's inner woman, whereas the latter is the woman's inner man. These elements have the potential to inspire the ego in order to perform the journey through and beyond the realm of the shadow. Fourth, is the "self"; it is the essential archetype, that of accomplishment of potential and the integration of personality. Usually, this archetype is represented by a mandala or magic circle, and it signifies the psychic totality towards which all life moves.

Undeniably, this means that the journey from ego to self is circular, implying the descent into the darkness of the shadow and the ascent towards the light of the self. Jung also considers that there is one archetype for each human situation, such as the child, the mother, the father, the hero, the trickster, the divine saviour, and others:

> They are repeated in all mythologies, fairy tales, religions, traditions, and mysteries. What else is the myth of the night sea voyage, of the wandering hero, or of the sea monster than our timeless knowledge transformed into a picture of the sun's setting and rebirth (...) Prometheus, the stealing of fire, Hercules, the slayer of dragons, the numerous myths of creation (...) and many other myths and tales portray psychic process in symbolic imaginary form. (Jacobi, 1951, p. 62)

For Jung, myths are not just some allegorical expressions of the natural phenomena; they represent the symbols of inner, unconscious world which could be accessed through projection and telling. He defines myths as "narrative elaboration of archetypal images" (Walker, 1992, p. 18). In his opinion, the mind grows aware of the archetypal image and engages itself in mythmaking, myth being "the natural and indispensable intermediate stage between unconscious and conscious cognition" (Walker, 1992, p. 19).

Myths reveal some fundamental messages, at the same time offering insights into unrealized or neglected aspects of human personality and forewarning the imbalance or the wrong action. As such, mythology becomes a mere "mirror of the collective unconscious" (Walker, 1992, p. 5).

Of course, this theory runs a great risk, since it may signify nothing but the denial of our freedom. Jung's theory threatens to reduce all our behaviour and, especially, all our literature to a known and well recognizable (archetypal) pattern in the collective psyche. This means that all situations are composed of some invariable or barely variable elements. Every generation of humanity exhausts itself in its attempt to reformulate these invariable elements and drains itself while writing down new lines found in the same ancient works.

This assumption leads to the idea that all great works of world literature are cyclical and Louis de Bernières' novel can be considered as a fraction of the same cycle.

However, Jung disputes the determinist aspect of archetypes, insisting that they are not determined in their content but in their form, and even this to a small degree. They present an "empty" structure, the substance of which is being filled by the matter of conscious experience and which, as a result, varies in each new manifestation. The power of archetypes lies in their structure rather than in their content, as the structure is transhistorical, whereas the content is appropriate only for a certain period and background. Therefore, myths and fairy tales that we inherit are mere expressions of the archetypes which have obtained specific features of the time in which they were written.

To sum up, Jung believes that myths are our expressions of the archetypes inborn in all of us, as our inheritance and part in the collective unconscious. The most important function of myth, in his opinion, is "to reveal the existence of the unconscious, to provide guidance in dealing with the unconscious, and to open the individual up to the unconscious and its wisdom" (Rochelle, 2000, p. 19).

Myth reveals essential truths about human condition in an emblematic language, and we become aware of these truths in this language and in the narrative of myth. Through story and language, myths manage to tap the human psyche, which is a gigantic, infinite depository of all knowledge about man and his relation to Divinity. Universal knowledge becomes available as individual knowledge only through the realm of myth.

There are some difficulties in applying Jung's sequence of archetypes to Louis de Bernières' novel, since in the case of a number of characters, there is a journey which is performed. This journey acquires the significance of an accomplishment of a potential and the integration of personality; sometimes, it takes the aspect of a physical motion; some other times, there is just a psychic movement of the character.

It is relatively easy to identify Corelli with Ulysses and his archetypal journey which de Bernières' protagonist has to perform, a journey which is both physical and psychological, and which conventionally implies the character's descent into inferno (or, in Jungian terms, the descent into the world of the shadow), where he encounters many demonic doubles of himself and even sees the greatest shadow of all, that is Satan/Evil. Then, reaching his anima – Pelagia (Penelope) – he becomes able to ascend from the abyssal darkness and attain a total vision of the cosmos and of his place within it.

The difficulty of approach to the novel emerges when we understand the writer's willingness to avoid the possible entrapment into a mythical situation or into an archetypal pattern, and his desire to deconstruct this well-known Odyssean formula. The postmodern Odysseus performs the journey, but does not achieve any material success; his anima is not encountered on his return home, but during the journey on a mysterious island, reminding us about Ulysses' bitter-sweet imprisonments by Circe and Calypso (negative animas); and the twenty years separation of Odysseus and Penelope has lasted for about fifty years in de Bernières' novel. Eventually, the mandala or magic circle, which signifies the psychic totality towards which all life moves, is not entirely completed by the protagonist, and is replaced by a spiral, since at the end of his odyssey he does not go home, but returns to the mysterious island and the woman of the island, who is his feminine counterpart, his journey being repeated several times.

However, we may hypothesize that, in the case of Corelli, each journey from ego to self is circular, involving descent into the darkness of the shadow and ascent towards the light of the self. Here we can even make a clearly discernible parallel with James George Frazer's cycle of the dying and reviving god, or with Eliade's eternal return, by which cosmos emerges from chaos. In de Bernières' work, however, the ultimate representation is the psychological integration.

The situation grows in complexity when the writer uses well recognizable prototypes in order to explore them and explode the meaning of myth and momomyth in an original manner, where a predictable situation or character typology is transformed into a completely different one, creating new connotations and gaining a new significance.

In Louis de Bernières' novel, myth acquires a kind of "protean" characteristic, preventing the creation of predictable meanings or expected outcomes in well-known situations; instead, the mythical situation or the archetypal pattern is perpetually renewed and reloaded with new meanings.

Consequently, the well-known Odyssean formula as completed by Odysseus and Penelope takes at certain instants the shape of Paris and Helen of Troy, Hector and Andromaque, Osiris and Isis, Eros and Psyche, Hades and Persephone, or Orpheus and Eurydice.

Orpheus myth is important to our reading through archetypal patterns, since Orpheus/Corelli is a musician and an artist who also goes to the underworld in order to bring back Eurydice/Pelagia, in Jungian terms, his anima, from the dead. Orpheus' material failure leads to his spiritual success, as Corelli's first loss of Pelagia leads to the composition of Pelagia's March, his music symbolizing also the attainment of the cosmic harmony. It is worth mentioning here de Bernières' attempt to deconstruct this archetypal pattern, when, like Orpheus after being dismembered by angry women, Corelli – here his body is torn out by the bullets of the Nazi soldiers – is saved from death by a woman, Pelagia, who assumes the role of Circe, a sorceress with knowledge of medicine.

At the same time, Corelli's resurrection leads us to another recognizable prototype, which is that of Jesus Christ, especially when the dismemberment/crucifixion similarity is completed by the fact that in both cases the material failure leads to spiritual success. But since we mention the "protean" characteristic of myth in Louis de Bernières novel, one cannot expect the creation of predictable meanings or expected outcomes in these well-known situations.

Similar interpretative perspectives can be discovered concerning other characters and situations involving these characters, as to name just Pelagia, Mandras, and Carlos, who, at different times, assume diverse archetypal roles, transforming the invariable mythical situations into other, unpredictable ones, gaining each time new connotations and new meanings.

In this respect, the Jungian theory of archetypes provides us with a useful pattern of analysis which is to be considered when it is revealed that the author makes appeal to this pattern, and, we may say, it must also be regarded when the author deconstructs it, since the rejection of a model presupposes a very good knowledge of it. In other words, it is essential to know and properly understand Jung's perspective in order to identify it when the text reveals it as used by de Bernières, as well as to apply it to the reading of de Bernières' text. It is also necessary to know the theory in order to understand how much Louis de Bernières deviates from a known archetype or replaces it with another one, and thus, in an intertextual perspective, reaching new symbolical significance and meaning.

1.3 Joseph Campbell

It is necessary to outline Joseph Campbell's understanding of myth, since Louis de Bernières focuses and relies heavily on some of Campbell's key concepts, among which is that of "the Monomyth of the Hero and the Quest". Although Campbell rejects to be classified as Jungian, his definitions of myth bear a resemblance to Carl Jung's ideas. Campbell accepts that the closest to a proper comprehension of the real significance of myth is Jung. In his description of myth, Campbell sounds much Jungian, because for him

> myths are telling us in picture language of powers of the psyche to be recognized and integrated in our lives (…). Thus they have not been, and can never be, displaced by the findings of science, which relate rather to the outside world than to the depths we enter in sleep. (Segal, 1987, p. 125)

Campbell, like Jung, embarks on a specifically psychological approach to myth. For him, myths are analogous to dreams and must be considered as seriously as dreams are. Myths provide access to the insight of the collective psyche or the collective soul, and the mere attempt to repress or disregard them as illusory might be psychologically and spiritually damaging.

The knowledge about human being is provided through dreams and this knowledge cannot be corrupted by the conscious defence mechanisms. Myths serve the same purpose for cultures. Joseph Campbell, similar to Carl Jung, insists that we need myths and a mythical consciousness in the contemporary period in order to conceive of an idea about who we are, where self-knowledge and identity are concepts that go beyond simple name, origin, and geographical setting.

Myth is perceived as an essential instrument used for the understanding of human psychology and, at the same time, as a symbolic manifestation of the human relationship with the divine, the inexpressible, and the indefinable.

Campbell differs from Jung when he considers myth from a sociological and anthropological perspective. For him, myth explains, validates, and preserves society as it is. Myth is also vital and indispensable for the maintenance of this society. Campbell presents four fundamental functions of myth, as summarized in the following passage:

> to install and maintain a sense of awe and mystery before the world (…) to explain the world; [as] a mythology is a system of effect symbols, signs evoking and directing a psychic response; (…) to maintain the social order by giving divine justification to social practices and institutions; [and] most of all, to harmonize the individual with society, the cosmos, himself, [by linking] him with everything both outside and within. (Segal, 1987, p. 111)

According to Campbell, "the goal of early life was to live in constant consciousness of the spiritual principle" or the mythic, whereas the modern man's lack of interest and indifference to it is the main reason for the meaningless, purposeless and disconnecting manner of existence in the contemporary world (Campbell, 1988, p. 120).

Jung appreciates myth for being a key to understanding the unconscious, without placing value upon myth itself. Myth is important to Jung as a vehicle to individuals' attempts to open a part of their self. Campbell, on the contrary, insists that "to accept myth is to accept it wholly (…) [it is] to identify oneself in myth" (Segal, 1987, p. 132). The complete identification with the mythic, in the case of Campbell, turns out to be essential and satisfactory to deepest human fulfilment.

Far from having the aim of presenting the similarities and differences between these two scholars, we should point, however, that both Campbell and Jung attempt to see the universality of myths as truthful metaphors and also to relate them to our current level of knowledge and experience.

In fact, the universal language of myth and archetype and the universal psychic tendencies have resulted in the conception of such themes as creation, descent into the underworld, the perception of divinity, and the hero quest.

Campbell's concept of the monomyth of the hero and the quest, or, in other words, the hero myth, may be considered the perfect paradigm for this universality, since its fundamental meaning is "all is one".

In his research of the hero myth, Joseph Campbell relies heavily on Jungian studies of the archetype and uses a term coined by James Joyce, which is that of "monomyth". The protagonist of the monomyth seeks out something lost, and in that process he experiences various transformations.

The monomythic life is made up by some crucial moments of the hero's development, such as the separation from home, the adventure in the unfamiliar world (the initiation and trial), and the return with a new comprehension of human existence. This quest of the hero is framed by a proper beginning and ending. The value of the journey and the quest of the hero lies in its universality, since "every individual hero symbolizes all mankind" (Segal, 1987, p. 5).

A more detailed consideration of the monomyth and the different elements that compose it, is the substance of the next chapter about the text of the novel. For now, we can say that Louis de Bernières uses Joseph Campbell's model of the hero myth – the monomyth of the hero and the quest – in his novel, and he attempts, at the same time, to retell, revise, and rethink the well-known heroic mythical stories or scenarios, presenting his own point of view and bringing to the centre of our attention some things and aspects neglected by us for a long time.

The focus of our research is placed exactly on the exploration of the ways in which Louis de Bernières revises and reimagines the monomyth, his reshaping of it taking, at times, a more radical form. While inverting the pattern of the hero myth and redefining its hero, de Bernières both justifies the primeval truths as expressed by myth and makes inquiries into myth.

To go from Corelli, a musician forced to become a soldier, to Pelagia, a young lady taking care of her father's household but having the ambition of becoming a doctor and a writer, is a matter of the author's purpose to redefine the monomyth and its hero in terms of gender, social hierarchy, historical background, morality, and the issue concerning the nature of the quest.

Presumably, Louis de Bernières wishes to dispute the ancient truths of the hero myth. The myth of the hero and his journey presents a pattern of human development, implying the growth of the self succeeding initiation and trial.

However, de Bernières becomes inquisitive about the meaning of this individual growth. He presents us with few types of hero, questioning the notion of courage and the value of quest during the war and at peace, at the same time revealing a different type – a domestic hero (both male and female) – whose courage and quest should be also evaluated, even though a journey was not performed. The British novelist invites us to rethink the deeds performed by humans in private or public, which are of no less importance.

Louis de Bernières stresses that there is more than one type of heroic action which also requires courage and stoicism, such as experiences of daily life, helping and nursing people, composing a melody or writing history. To conclude, de Bernières assumes Campbell's paradigm of the mythic hero, but warns us that there might be more than one way of being heroic, more than one nature of heroic quest, whether in private or public environment.

1.4 Claude Lévi-Strauss

One way of making a distinction between early twentieth century approaches to myth and more recent studies is to consider the former as concerned with the establishing of the origin and the latter as preoccupied primarily with the structure and functions of myth.

Claude Lévi-Strauss refuses to believe in the sacredness of myth or in the language of the gods speaking through myth. For him, in *Le Cru et le Cuit* (1964), "myths have no author: as soon as they are perceived as myths, whatever their actual origin may have been, they exist only embodied in a tradition. When a myth is told, individual listeners receive a message that properly speaking comes from nowhere" (Lévi-Strauss cited in Brunel, 1992, p. xi).

Lévi-Strauss, throughout a long career of research, investigated thousands of myths from all over the world seeking to determine their common format. He refuses to accept the idea of myth as originating in a "primitive" mind, insisting that myth exhibits a rigorous level of thinking, similar to the one found in modern science.

Lévi-Strauss relies on structural linguistics in his attempt to examine the composition of myth. To him, the structures of myth suggest that the structures of the human mind are common to all people. Myth, in his opinion, is nothing else than a fundamental and original category of the human mind, which is in contact with rational and logical thinking, that is, the mythic thought. This mythic thought, which is advanced by succeeding dichotomies and oppositions, is able to diminish both reality and itself to a simple universal network.

Myth and thought are therefore not dependent upon any historical circumstance. Embodying the first and the most intense expression of the mind, myth and thought are actually of the same essence with it, as with language, with which they undeniably have many morphological similarities.

In this way, myth becomes a language, a universal narrative pattern that exceeds the cultural and temporal barriers, and speaks to all people. Lévi-Strauss suggests that the substance of myth is not contained in its style or syntax, but in the story it tells, in the way in which its constituent elements or mythemes mingle together to create meaning. Lévi-Strauss continues by asserting the structure of myth as a development from the awareness of opposites to their resolution, emphasizing that it is this aspect that confers energy to a myth as it transforms, mutates, and alters through a variety of its telling.

Claude Lévi-Strauss considers this transformative capacity of myth as an essential factor:

> a myth, or a group of myths, far from constituting an inert corpus subject to pure mechanical influences operating by means of the addition or subtraction of discrete elements, must be defined, in a dynamic perspective, as one particular state of a transformational group, temporarily in equilibrium with other states, and whose apparent stability depends, on a superficial level, on the degree to which the tensions prevailing between two states cancel each other out. (Lévi-Strauss, 1990, pp. 208–209)

The mythic thought functions, according to Lévi-Strauss, primarily through the process of transformation, which is given as much importance as to structure. The transformation and the structure, relying constantly upon each other, represent the two foremost modalities by which mythic thought becomes apparent.

Daniel Dubuisson, in his work *Twentieth Century Mythologies*, discusses the mutually supportive aspect of transformation and structure, which is essential for the manifestation of the mythic thought. He claims that "if structural analysis seems to favour the discovery of stable relations and states, transformation does not so much introduce brutal and unforeseeable changes as exploit dynamic combinations governed by a system of rules" (Dubuisson, 2006, p. 130).

Consequently, in interpreting myth, we can never refer to a single symbol, but to the overall structure; not to its significance for the individual, but to collective logic which is implicit. The creative perception of the writer revises the primary structure of myth, transforming it through alterations and through mythemes, and creating an original symbolic situation as a new mythological as well as literary tradition which includes new thematic perspectives, character representation strategies, and techniques for the structural organization of the text.

The representation of reality as revealed by myth is achieved through a distinct structural framework which is unique to myth. In our study, we attempt to disclose the mechanisms through which some established mythical meanings are transformed. This aspect becomes essential especially in the postmodern era, in which the well-known mythical meanings are altered or deconstructed in order to convey a new relevant meaning pertinent to the contemporary milieu.

As mentioned above, Lévi-Strauss insists that "myth is language" and it might be considered a premise in our study, namely that myth, in the writings of Louis de Bernières, possesses the same values and functions as language does. Myth is a system of signs and mythemes which perpetually recombine and transform the pre-existing mythological constituent into a new system.

The newly emerged system reveals the capacity of the same elements to appear in another form, even in an inverted one, but, eventually, following the course of some successive transformations through a sufficiently extensive body of myths, this change reveals primarily the relationship, the inverted symmetry, the isomorphous resemblance to the previous system.

The structural approach to Louis de Bernières' novel is revelatory to our study, since we consider that the British novelist uses some mythical structures and mythemes from the well-known situations, like the Trojan war, the Trojan horse, the flames of burning Troy, the hero's journey and quest, friendship, rivalry, the poet's quest, the descent of the hero into the underworld, the descent of gods to earth, etc., recombining and transforming their mythological elements into a new system which possesses validity for the universal and contemporary cultural codes.

This newly materialized system, which is de Bernières' novel, proves the efficiency of the same mythemes to come into view in another form, such as the Second World War, the dispute of supreme powers during the Nazi regime, the flames of the burning bodies of soldiers on the Greek island, friendship as true love of a friend, but also implying a homosexual aspect, as well as the warrior as primarily a poet, the hero's journey and quest materialized into the composition of a march, enemy spies dropping down to earth instead of descending gods, and many other changed mythemes.

At the same time, Louis de Bernières inverts some units of myth, as when Mandras, in a typical heroic manner, performs a journey and a quest, and emerges completely transformed, especially by his newly acquired ability of reading, but, ironically, instead of achieving the expected spiritual growth or harmony, he emerges as a degraded individual, a rapist whose prior ideals have been completely corrupted by the totalitarian mirages. However, following the trajectory of these successive transformations through an adequate number of mythemes as units of myths, this change discloses the correlation and resemblance to the previous system.

Myth, accepted as a structural system, assumes the existence of a centre or an origin (mytheme), which is both universal and contemporary.

Louis de Bernières challenges his reader to discover this centre or mytheme, but, once found, it becomes dislocated, constantly transferring to another system, revealing the capacity of a mytheme to render continuously numerous meanings and proving continuously its protean attributes. This transformative quality of myth becomes fundamental, especially in the context of postmodern mythical meta-narratives, where the previously established structures and meanings become deconstructed, since no absolute truth or certainty is ever validated.

Louis de Bernières' fiction, understood as a structural system, allows the transformation of mythical units into an ultimately postmodern form whose lack of an established meaning engages the reader into the privileged role of author himself in order to create his or her own meaning and significance according to his or her own cultural code, while restricting or accepting the established meanings of the modern mythical discourse.

1.5 Roland Barthes

One of the most influential European thinkers of the second half of the twentieth century, Roland Barthes, also relies on structural linguistics in his exploration of myth. To Barthes, myth is envisaged as "a type of speech" that communicates a message; he claims that "myth is not defined by the object of its message, but by the way in which it utters this message" (Barthes, 1991, p. 109).

Therefore, myth is not characterized by its message or purpose, but by the particular way or form in which the message manages to convey a meaning. Barthes demystifies myth completely by presenting it as a specific system of communication. He depicts myth as "a second-order semiological system" (Barthes, 1991, p. 114), a definition which relies on Ferdinand de Saussure's pattern of language as a tridimensional structure, more exactly the signifier, the signified, and the sign, comprising the concept to be articulated, an acoustic or graphic form corresponding to the concept, and the relation between both of them.

Barthes insists that this model is found in myth, but with an essential distinction that is created upon an already established linguistic conjunction. That is to say, myth emerges from an existing correlation between concept and form, on which it then imposes its own auxiliary system of signification. Barthes insists upon this auxiliary system of signification, since its connotation depends on the way in which it is perceived as well as on the context.

In other words, the same sign gains different connotations at a different time and/or in different situations. Also, one should consider the possibility of several signs to carry the same connotation, conveying similar meanings. Given that the connotation or the second-order meaning results from association of ideas, it may become ideologically loaded, stemming from the vision of the worldview that we share with people from the same social, historical and cultural background, and may, therefore, be based on convention.

The arbitrary nature of the sign has been long ago acknowledged by Ferdinand de Saussure, who stresses that the association between signifier and signified is not based on natural resemblance, but on convention. It is this conventional aspect of myth that Barthes tries to emphasize when he struggles to show that our daily life is riddled with myths based on cultural conventions and that the purpose of these myths is to make us confuse culture for nature.

This attempt of transforming the meaning into form is called by Barthes as "language-robbery", and it confers to myth its richness, and makes it seem more natural when its oppressive implications are veiled and the primary signification is superimposed with new directives (Barthes, 1991, pp. 131–132). In this respect, Barthes writes: "One could say that a language offers to myth an open-work meaning. Myth can easily insinuate itself into it, and swell there: it is a robbery by colonization. (…) Myth can reach everything, corrupt everything" (Barthes, 1991, p. 132).

Roland Barthes reveals this distinctive capacity of myth with the purpose to transform the meanings according to the dominant cultural code. Myth acts on already established signs or first order denotative systems.

The connotative mythical sign of the second-order meaning extends the area of expression according to the peculiarities of the culture within which it operates. However, myth does not exert its power only in the second-order meaning. A third-order meaning should be considered as an auxiliary system of signification, which is achieved through the inversions and re-contextualization of myth.

Myth emerges out of this semiologic process tremendously distorted and its capacity to represent a reality is altered as well. We should also specify that the author is not the only factor contributing to the creation of this auxiliary system of signification; the reader contributes as well to the supplementation of meaning. Consequently, the modified meaning of myth originates and becomes transformed on an individual ground.

In *Captain Corelli's Mandolin*, Louis de Bernières makes extensive use of Roland Barthes' theories when he tries to explore and, at the same time, to warn his readers about the dangers of the plurality of meanings, which is confusing and attests, in a way, the failure of reason to grasp the reality. The best way to explain this phenomenon is to present some examples from the novel.

The first illustration would be provided by Mandras, the young fisherman from the Greek island. After the participation in the liberating war, he, together with all islanders, must experience the oppression of the fascists. As it is given in the novel, "all they knew was that they were driven by something from the very depths of the soul, something that commanded them to rid their land of strangers or die in the attempt" (De Bernières, 1995, p. 228).

All these people, obviously, have a common desire, which is liberation. This word's denotation or the first-order meaning refers to the act of freeing the island from foreign occupation. The connotation or the second-order meaning, in Mandras' mind, is associated with the myth of freedom, equality, Promised Land, or a magical utopia achieved by him for his people. When this concept assumes a form, which is communism, an auxiliary system of signification is imposed upon it, and it becomes ideologically loaded.

This ideological semiology stems from the worldview that the character shares with the people from the same cultural, social and historical background, and which seems to be logical at that time. Consequently, the connotative association in Mandras' mind of the concept "liberation" with the form "communism" is not based on conviction but on convention.

We can say that Mandras becomes a victim of the so-called "language-robbery" that occurs when the association of the meaning appears to him as natural, whereas its oppressive implications are veiled and the primary signification is superimposed with new directives. In Mandras' case, the relation that unites the concept of myth to its meaning is essentially a relation of "deformation", to use Barthes' term, since a formal analogy is being made with a complex semiological system.

This type of analogy is not just misleading, but it also becomes dangerous, because it does not simply corrupt the initial meaning of the concept; by extension, this phenomenon has a tremendous impact, because it corrupts the individual's worldview, and, in Mandras' case, it also corrupts his soul. At first Mandras takes pleasure in this metonymic association with communism, since it appears to stimulate every aspect of his life and to nurture his transformation. He learns reading, has the impression of doing something extremely useful for his community, and considers the organization and principles of the communists to function as liberating.

However, a possible third-order meaning should be taken into consideration, which supplements the system of signification, and which is achieved through the inversions and re-contextualization of myth. Instead of a communist hero-liberator having as his major priority the welfare, equality, and freedom of his community, we are confronted with Mandras the oppressor of his own people, who makes his own justice and is convinced of his righteousness. Mandras' enthusiastic appartenance to communism simply marks his personal degradation which leads later to his monstrous transformation into a new capacity as murderer and rapist.

This example illustrates how myth emerges out of this semiologic process as greatly distorted, while its ability to represent a reality is altered as well.

The same could be said about the young German soldier Günter Weber. He becomes a Nazi trusting the denotation of this word which implies a master race, a superior nation. But the connotation or the second-order meaning in Günter's case is associated with the Aryan myth of Nordic warriors, which is supposed to refer to a race superior in physical aspect as well as in intelligence.

The supplemented system of signification allows the rise of the ideological implication applied to the word, leading to the creation of an icon of the blond-haired, blue-eyed, intelligently superior individual-warrior who is justified to rule above other inferior races and is even fit to exterminate them. The young Günter relies on the convention of this Aryan myth when he desperately tries to look like one of these superior specimens. For this reason, he frequently takes sunbaths "hoping that sun would bleach his hair. But there was nothing he could do to transform his brown eyes to an unsuspiciously Aryan blue" (De Bernières, 1995, p. 240).

Weber's sympathetic attitude towards Nazism is developed not on personal conviction, but from the Third Reich's revitalization of the impact of past mythologies. The novelist, through his narrator, says: "Weber was still a virgin, his father was a Lutheran pastor, and he had grown up in the Austrian mountains, capable of hating Jews and gypsies only because he had never met one" (De Bernières, 1995, p. 243).

As mentioned above, such an ideological semiology appears again from the view on existence that the character shares with other people from the same milieu, and it seems to be based on convention.

But, as in the case of Mandras, this plurality of meaning leads to fundamental transformations of this young man. Instead of fulfilling his dreams of becoming a superior human, Günter Weber must turn into a tool of limitless cruelty and inhumanity mastered by his cultural code.

The third-order meaning which supplements the system of signification is created around this malignant inversion and it gains more intensity by Weber's image of lost virginity/innocence in a kind of metaphorical paedophilia enacted by the ideology of the Third Reich.

Captain Corelli's Mandolin is a work in which Louis de Bernières takes the opportunity to explore the dangers of the plurality of meanings which are derived by the same linguistic sign, and to scrutinize the impact that this phenomenon creates upon individual lives and upon our worldview, as to eventually indicate, in a way, the failure of language to express reality.

2. Practical Argumentation

2.1 Rethinking the Monomyth of the Hero and the Quest as a Critical Concern

The contemporary world we live in differs much from the more or less romantic heroic illusions of the preceding centuries. The human experience, including its heroic dimension, is in a perpetual flux, a continuous process of transformation. This process of mutability is both conscious and unconscious. In this context, it seems that myth appears as a needed authority from the unconscious realm which releases "the common darkness", well-known archetypal images as heroes, monsters, quests, trials, objects of power, journeys, and returns.

Created by the collective imagination, or the Great Anonymous, as Mircea Eliade puts it, myths mostly represent the projections of the manner in which the things exist in life, and are, for the most part, related to our current level of knowledge and experience. As David Leeming states, "myths emerge from our experience of reality (…) from our instinctive need to cloth that experience in mimetic story and concept" (Leeming, 2001, pp. 19–20).

However, we are also aware that our experiences as well as cultures change in the passage of time. Myths, as part of our experience and culture, must be subject to change in order to become useful to us in the process of sharing knowledge and experience. In other words, in order to avoid their decay into obsoleteness which might impede the transmission of a message, myths need to be revised, retold or reimagined according to the aim and intention of the teller or according to the necessity and tastes of the audience of a certain cultural and historical milieu. In this process of retelling or reimagining of myth, our relation to the whole picture of existence becomes re-examined, re-evaluated, as it comes to meet the changing cultural conditions, depending on the domination, censorship, morals or ideologies of our contemporary world.

Therefore, in this process of retelling of myth, some earlier neglected aspects of a certain myth could be revived or transformed, leading to the discovery of some new, earlier unexplored aspects, meanings, points of view, or bringing to the centre of attention some characters and creatures earlier ignored or forgotten.

Louis de Bernières writes his novel *Captain Corelli's Mandolin* in a period of radical changes in the history of humanity, changes which affect drastically the imaginative world of the artists excelling in that period. De Bernières and other contemporary writers enjoy considerable latitude in altering or retelling myths to fit their own purposes and in this way providing, in the process of their retelling, fundamental but surprising and fascinating perspectives.

Louis de Bernières' artistic imagination interacts for the most part with the monomyth of the hero and the quest, and through it with the Homeric mythico-heroic scenario of *Iliad* and *Odyssey*, and also with other literary traditions of Antiquity, which explore myth at great length, like Virgil's *Aeneid* and Ovid's *Metamorphoses*, treating them with great liberty. At the same time, the novelist focuses on Biblical myth and changes the content of the consolidated myth through a diversification and innovation of the themes, ideas, representation of characters, values, and theories.

Concurrently with the well-known myths, de Bernières uses his creative freedom to investigate some other, more recent mythical scenarios, among which the Aryan myth, the Dictator myth, and the totalitarian myth are worth mentioning.

However, what mostly attracts our attention is the novelist's intention of retelling the hero myth, or, in Campbell's terms, the monomyth of the hero and the quest.

In his endeavour, de Bernières tries to preserve the structural elements of the monomyth, and, at the same time, create a coherent, normative and dynamic literary system which emerges as depending on some requirements or on specific inner parameters. Concomitantly, the newly evolved literary system is in a continuous transformation due to the varying visions of the writer concerning the concept of heroism in the postmodern age.

In particular, the emphasis is placed by the novelist on the different types of courage, as well as on various manners of being brave or heroic in the contemporary world.

In referring to de Bernières' attempt to retell or reimagine the hero myth, we consider Joseph Campbell's concept of monomyth, or the hero-myth and the quest, which functions as a structure upon which the novelist applies his variations. As every structure, the monomyth tends to be static, providing a typological concept of existence within a community, which, as a consequence, becomes identifiable or identified and particularized. However, as every myth, the monomyth of the hero and the quest tends to take on a new, dramatic and dynamic character when artistic imagination is involved, providing thus the possibility for revision, radical reshaping, or inversion of the mythic essence.

We assume that the monomyth of the hero and the quest, or the hero-myth, represents a complex and dynamic literary system framed within a unified literary tradition and typology as thematic matter and structural expression. That is why the typology and the dynamics of the hero-myth deserve a close investigation in the postmodern background, a context within which Louis de Bernières has operated. Yet, prior to our exploration of de Bernières' heroes and heroic pattern, we should have a closer look at Joseph Campbell's consideration of the monomyth of the hero and the quest, and only afterwards try to explain the need for its revival and revision in the postmodern context.

After all, as Pierre Brunel has aptly noted, "no literary myth arises unless there is a regeneration that conjures the myth back to life at a given period, demonstrating its capacity to express pertinently the problems of that age" (Brunel, 1992, p. xiii). Even though we deal with reshaping or inversion of a myth, the symbolical references to that myth reveal in the best possible way the stringent problems of the community which re-creates it.

2.2 The Paradigm of the Monomyth of the Hero and the Quest in Joseph Campbell's Conception

The hero's journey as a paradigm was presented by the mythologist Joseph Campbell in his renowned work *The Hero with a Thousand Faces* (1949). To speak about the journey of the hero, in this book he introduces the term "monomyth" using a word which was coined earlier by James Joyce, whom Campbell highly valued, in *Finnegans Wake* (1939): "And then and too the trivials! And their bivouac! And his monomyth! Ah ho! Say no more about it! I'm sorry! I saw. I'm sorry! I'm sorry to say I saw!"

Quoting Joyce, Campbell defines monomyth as an everlasting reiteration in the framework of one narrative of unchanging principles and events inflected in a particular and unique way. The principles and events are unique and representative for each individual, since the hero of the monomyth is our representative of the self, and the monomyth is the journey of each of us as an individual. We cannot experience someone else's narrative, and our story is a particular myth framed as a metaphor or allegory of the agony of self-completion through the control over and assimilation of conflicting opposite principles.

The archetypal hero is the substance of the monomyth representing a process of various symbolic elements or adventures, such as trials, quests, encounters, and so on, having a transformative essence and consisting of the totality of individual and collective consciousness and unconscious.

Thus, in the attempt to present this heroic model and explain it, one should rely on both Joseph Campbell's and Carl Jung's approaches, since Campbell's definition of the monomyth with its separate phases depends much on Jung's psychological method which employs archetypes.

Campbell explains that the monomyth refers to a hero's and less often a heroine's journey that could be found in all communities. He observes that the hero of various societies passes through different phases of a journey of self-empowerment and self-recognition that should transform forever both the hero and the citadel.

Campbell associates the hero's journey to the rituals of passage from childhood to adulthood in which young people take responsibilities in their community. He claims that "the standard path of the mythological adventure of the hero is a magnification of the formula represented in the rites of passage: *separation – initiation – return*: which might be named the nuclear unit of the monomyth" (Campbell, 1968, p. 30).

These essential stages define the monomythic life: the departure from the native environment, the adventure in the unfamiliar world, and the return with a new awareness of the world. This tripartite heroic experience is framed by a proper beginning and ending.

We perceive the hero's journey as a powerful and recurring archetype which is deeply enrooted in human psyche and therefore fundamental to human existence. This hero's journey corresponds to a process of individual development from a disjointed sense of identity to a consolidated identity, when the individual acquires a clear sense of aspiration in life. In other words, the monomyth reveals human experience, in particular the process of maturation of an individual, the reaching and acknowledgment of the adult self.

The first phase in Campbell's heroic pattern is separation, which Campbell names as "call to adventure". This stage corresponds to the hero's dissatisfaction with the predominant values of his community. The hero's separation from his home and familiar environment is both physical and psychic when he decides to discover a superior value system by which he is determined to live.

Campbell explains the role of this first stage as "a radical transfer of emphasis from the external to the internal world, macro- to microcosms, a retreat from the desperation of the waste land to the peace of the everlasting realm that is within" (Campbell, 1968, p. 17). In this process of the hero's fundamental retreat into an inner world, he discovers his unknown and latent potential of becoming an individual of great importance.

Erich Neumann, one of the most creative Jungians, depicts this segment in the human development as "the history of [the] self-emancipation of the ego struggling to free itself from the powers of unconscious to hold its own against overwhelming odds" (Neumann cited in Noel, 1991, p. 206).

Joseph Henderson, another disciple of Jung, explains that this heroic stage corresponds to "the development of the individual's ego-consciousness", a moment when the human being apprehends his own potency and weakness in "a manner that will equip him for the arduous tasks with which life confronts him (…). The image of the hero evolves in a manner that reflects each stage of the evolution of the human personality" (Henderson, 1964, p. 112).

The call to adventure is not necessarily followed by an eager or enthusiastic attitude of the hero. On the contrary, the hero might be reluctant to separate from home with all its comforts. The Homeric protagonist Odysseus, for example, is not willing to abandon his wife, his son and Ithaca in order to accept the call of the Achaeans to sake Troy, and, to avoid it, pretends madness at first. Achilles is another hero who is reluctant to join the Trojan War, disguising himself into a young girl in order to avoid the callers. Eventually, the hero acknowledges that there is no way of living perpetually in the same mode, some old principles should be revised, and a new system of values should be achieved. As a result, to attain renewal through journey and adventure, the hero departs from home to seek eternal glory.

From a psychological perspective, this stepping out of a familiar world provides the possibility for the young man to cross the threshold of the adventure of adulthood, which signifies the formation of a complete personality and the acquiring of a satisfying life.

The second stage, which is that of initiation and testing, is marked by some dreadful challenges that the hero must undergo to confirm his worth. The hero's journey denotes various archetypal patterns, and among the most important ones is that of the quest. Usually, the nature of the hero's call determines the object of his quest. The hero may search for someone lost, as Odysseus seeks for his son Telemachus, or Theseus tries to find his father, or Orpheus searches for his wife Eurydice. There might be an object to be found by the hero, as the quest for the Holy Grail of the Knights of the Round Table, or Jason's search for the Golden Fleece. Then, the hero may look for a place, like Moses' quest for the Promised Land. Also, the hero may have an intangible task, like Jesus who searches for the Kingdom of God. As Campbell explains,

> there are two types of deed. One is physical deed, in which the hero performs a courageous act in battle or saves a life. The other kind is the spiritual deed, in which the hero learns to experience the supernormal range of human spiritual life and then comes back with a message. (Campbell, 1968, p. 152)

The initiation is a significant part of the hero's quest, since the hero-to-become is still a novice in a hostile foreign environment, and his being guided and assisted by an older or wiser person as a parental figure is fundamental for his success.

The form of initiation differs from hero to hero: some young men are taught the skill of fighting, or the secret of ancient letters, or the manner of slaying a dragon, like Sigurd; others are given wise advises, like Jason or Arthur; others are helped by their divine tutors to determine the tasks they should perform in order to accomplish their quest, like Odysseus. Frequently, the assistants of the hero possess superior knowledge and/or some magical powers, like Regin, Medea, Merlin, and Calypso. As a result of sorcery and the newly gained skill and wisdom, the hero manages to succeed in his endeavours.

From a psychological perspective, this episode from the hero's adventure corresponds to the young adult's initial stages of journey into adulthood when both the physical and spiritual deeds are necessary to accomplish his quest. The physical deed could represent the completion of physiological ripeness of an individual, since this maturation phase includes also the acknowledgment and practice of sexuality.

However, the maturation process could not be completed without psychic and spiritual maturity. The young man must overcome a disjointed sense of identity that nurtures self-doubt and should determine the purpose of his life. It is now that the young man needs the support of tutors, friends, and assistants who would lead him wisely in his journey. This stage represents the essential part of the hero's journey, since, during the adventures, in addition to this segment, the hero discovers his identity.

The process of self-discovery is greatly stimulated by the difficult trials that the hero must undergo throughout his quest. A dragon should be slain, a giant should be defeated, a guardian to be tricked, or an anti-hero should be overpowered at every threshold that the hero must traverse. These trials happen in the yet unknown environment, in which the hero may find himself in a "dream landscape of curiously fluid ambiguous forms" (Campbell, 1968, p. 97).

In this marvellous environment, the hero's trials represent the testing of his body, spirit, and mind. In Jungian terms, the episode of trials represents the challenge of complexes of the personal unconscious, which impede the growth and self-realization of the individual. The Jungian notion of the shadow becomes significant in this context, as it represents, in archetypal terms, the totality of all impediments met by the personal unconscious in the process of self-discovery.

The shadow, considered mostly as the negative or dark aspect of the unconscious, should be confronted by the ego in order to achieve the self-knowledge of the individual. By recognizing and then by confronting his negative characteristics, the individual prevents their projection onto others. The slaying of the dragon and the defeating of a giant represent mere attempts of the ego to confront the dark side of one's self, where the victory of the hero over the beast may symbolize his victory over power of the shadow. By slaying the inner dragons, or, in other words, his negative aspects of identity, the hero passes the necessary test in the identity formation, which is essential in the process of development of an individual.

This process of internal transformation enables the hero to engage into the next stage of his quest. The new trial implies the encounter with the goddess, a phase which is important for the elevation and the self-confidence of the hero.

As Campbell suggests, this meeting with the goddess is "the bliss-bestowing goal of every Hero's earthly and unearthly Quest. [The Goddess] is mother, sister, mistress, bride" (Campbell, 1968, p. 111). The goddess is frequently depicted as beneficent, benevolent, compassionate, procreator, and nurturer. This maternal aspect of the goddess suggests an association with Mother Archetype which represents the creative universal powers that predominated once in the fertility cultures of Antiquity.

This central image of the Mother goddess had a fundamental impact upon the individuals living in agrarian communities. Campbell explains that

> it has to do with earth. The human woman gives birth just as the earth gives birth to the plants. She gives nourishment, as the plants do. So, woman magic and earth magic are the same. They are related. And the personification of the energy that gives birth to forms and nourishes forms is properly female. (Campbell and Moyers, 1988, p. 167)

Eventually, when fertility cultures became superseded by a warrior ethos brought by invading nomadic tribes, as a consequence of this fundamental cultural transformation, the powers of the goddess were considerably reduced. As the archetypal psychologist Jean Bolen suggests, "the Goddess (known by different names) became the subservient consort of the invader gods, and her attributes and powers were absorbed (swallowed) or came under the domination of a male deity" (Bolen, 1989, p. 298).

Most probably, as a result of these profound cultural changes revealed by the struggle of the Mother goddess with the male god, the image of the goddess has acquired some new aspects, such as *femme fatale*, unattainable or prohibited. The temptress devastates the patriarchal hero when she exerts her supremacy over him in order to overpower or test his strength. The seduction represents an archetypal image of the dangerous sexual and totally private alternative to the true purpose of the hero. The newly attained sexual knowledge may serve as a proof of the hero's masculinity which is important for the individual's growth. At the same time, it awakens the desire of an individual to be whole. The knowledge of femininity achieved by the hero (revealed in various forms) makes him aware that only heroic experience might not be satisfactory for his existence. The grace, the warmth and tranquillity may be alternative joys for the individual to achieve self-completion.

This encounter with the goddess during the hero's journey has the aim of awakening the dormant creative powers of the Mother archetype, which are beneficent to the hero and community. Campbell calls this encounter as the "sacred marriage" with the Mother Goddess. Jung also suggests that the "sacred marriage" reveals a psychological reunion with the Mother archetype, which stimulates a fundamental change of the individual. James Redfield develops further the importance of this encounter:

> [I]f we are to open up to the full potential of transpersonal awareness, we must become conscious of and integrate both the female and male aspects of our higher selves (...) [I]n order to connect with the divine energy within, we must locate, court, and finally engage the energy of the female nurturer within our own being. (Redfield, 1997, p. 160)

The essential function of the "sacred marriage" refers to the union of all archetypes of the unconscious and to the power and wisdom which are necessary to confront all the possible anxieties of the personal unconscious in order to allow the continuation of the hero's quest. According to Jung, the "sacred marriage" with the Mother archetype symbolizes the accomplishment of an integrated personality that incorporates various archetypes of the collective unconscious.

Consequently, the "sacred marriage" implies the fact that in order to become integrated and complete, the individual should be secure about Mother's absolute love. The confidence in love provides a solid ground which is essential for the accomplishment of psychological wholeness of the individual.

Following the encounter with the goddess, the hero should experience the atonement with the father. Various myths and mystical situations imply the centrality of the Father archetype in the psychological growth of a man. These myths and mystical experiences reveal a contrasting position to the one presented by Sigmund Freud in the example of the Oedipus complex, where the relationship between father and son is based on rivalry and competitiveness.

On the contrary, many of these stories narrate a rather cooperative and satisfying relationship between father and son or daughter. Definitely, in this relation, a certain examination is implied, since the father "[admits] to his house only those who have been thoroughly tested" (Campbell, 1968, p. 133). The father is not necessary the biological father, he could be a wise man, a paternal figure, or an "initiating priest through whom the young being passes on into the larger world" (Campbell, 1968, p. 136).

The encounter with the father is identified by Campbell as "atonement". The word "atonement" is not to be necessarily understood in the contemporary meaning of redemption. The older usage of the word, referring to regeneration or reconciliation, is of greater interest to us, as it suggests harmony and equilibrium. Consequently, the encounter with the father brings up the encounter with one's self, when an individual surpasses his personal desires and struggles to restore a lost kingdom – a self-actualized life (Campbell, 1968, p. 246).

In Jungian terms, the individual should traverse the transpersonal and transcultural reality in order to find himself. In his quest for self-identity, the individual should not simply explore, confront, and, at times, fight personal or cultural demon guardians of the gate, but is supposed to discover and bring into consciousness the Self, which is confined or deprived by those guardians.

The concept of the Self evolves from the Hindu Upanishads and refers to the inner expression of Brahman, which is the absolute infinite existence. In the tradition of the Upanishads, the ultimate experience (Nirvana) is to understand and achieve the sameness between the individual's immortal perfect spirit (Atman) and the absolute infinite existence (Brahman). The Brahman and Atman being One, the same is one as well. The acknowledgement of one's existence as a quintessence of the transpersonal world, as one's true Self, is the true heroic goal which goes beyond satisfaction or conquest.

The Self can be considered as an archetype of wholeness, which organizes and unifies the unconscious and the consciousness. It is the embodiment of individuality and a means by which one reunites with the great circle of life. The atonement with the father refers to the stage of re-joining the great circle of life, which means the discovery of one's place in the universe.

The dragon slaying, the sacred marriage, and the atonement with the father correspond to the archetypal encounters with the shadow, anima and self which are crucial for the union of the conscious and the unconscious of the individual psyche, and, as a consequence, for personal accomplishment and for understanding the meaning in life. These three archetypal meetings are fundamental in the process of self-discovery. The one who fails in these encounters remains a victim of the self-blocking factors, as neurosis or obsessions, which are formed in the course of one's life and which lead to the formation of a fragmented identity of the self.

When all the encounters are completed and the triumph over all the impediments is accomplished, the hero is prepared to take the ultimate boon, which could be the elixir of life, or the Golden Fleece, or the singing harp. But in order to complete his journey, the hero must return home and share the achieved gifts with his community, the return being the third stage of the hero's journey according to Campbell.

However, the monomythic hero is frequently reluctant to return to his world. The "refusal of return" refers to the dilemma of the hero who is not sure about homecoming. Since the return implies the sharing or teaching of wisdom, compassion and of the ultimate truth to an ignorant and critical society, the hero frequently reflects on the option of remaining enthralled in a nirvanic experience. Jung explains the refusal of return as the unwillingness to abandon the superior state of consciousness, which has been achieved in the course of the journey of self-discovery, and to re-join the ordinary waking consciousness.

In the "crossing the return threshold", the hero accepts eventually the necessity of his return, considering it an appealing opportunity to reform the moral vision of his world. The hero assumes the role of a moral guide, a progressive leader or a visionary prophet who transforms his world. The essential element in the hero's homecoming is that he has reached a synthesis of moral wisdom and worldly supremacy that will suffice in changing his community forever. According to Campbell, the return of the hero is compulsory. He explains that

> when the hero-quest has been accomplished through penetration to the source, or through the grace of some male or female, human or animal, personification, the adventurer still must return with his life-transmitting trophy. The full round, the norm of the monomyth, requires the hero should now begin the labour of bringing the runes of wisdom, the Golden Fleece, or his sleeping princess, back into the kingdom of humanity, where the boon may redound to the renewing of the community. (Campbell, 1968, p. 193)

And although the hero's journey might seem a linear process, Carol Pearson insists upon a cyclical fashion for the hero's experience:

> I will illustrate the typical hero's progression as a cone of three-dimensional spiral, in which it is possible to move forward while frequently circling back. Each stage has its own lesson to teach us, and we reencounter situations that throw us back into prior stages so that we may learn and relearn the lessons as new lessons at new levels of intellectual and emotional complexity and subtlety. (Pearson, 1989, p. 13)

But the cyclic process implies death. Thus, on their return home, some heroes must die or descend into the place of death, like scapegoats for the errors of the others. There are numberless examples of the hero's descent into the underworld which are followed by the image of return from the realm of death, as to mention just Orpheus, Hercules, Odysseus, and Aeneas; death, in a distinct manner, may be defeated as in the example of Jesus' resurrection.

The psychological dimension corresponding to the self-discovery process seems obvious: the "hero's journey to the underworld not only resembles both ancient, widespread initiation rites and a natural, probably almost universal human psychic experience, it satisfies a human need" (Lowry, 1982, p. 121). The hero emerges greatly transformed after this experience, learning the ultimate knowledge for the humans, which is that of death and rebirth. This supreme knowledge provides the psychic wholeness that the hero has sought during his long and demanding Quest.

2.3 Reimagining the Monomyth of the Hero and the Quest in *Captain Corelli's Mandolin*

Louis de Bernières' novel *Captain Corelli's Mandolin* fits clearly into the parameters of the monomyth. However, although de Bernières accepts the heroic pattern as presented by Jung and Campbell, he considers that some of its aspects require a reinterpretation. In his endeavour, the author is willing to show that the hero has definitely multiple hypostases. These multiple faces or aspects are revealed in the novel through the portrayal of distinct personages that suggest distinct aspects of human psyche. As the hero's hypostases vary throughout the novel, the hero's quests reveal some variations as well.

The motif of the journey is also revised, since some of the characters in de Bernières' novel show clearly the pattern of separation-adventure-return (Mandras); some characters are presented in the middle of their adventure, following the departure and ending with a return to the foreign land conceived as motherland (Corelli); others never move from their homeland but still perform a different kind of voyage to find their true self (Pelagia).

Moreover, Louis de Bernières' characters, his heroes and heroines with distinct faces, do not perform just one initiatory and self-fulfilling journey. The journey could be reiterated, until the hero manages to discover his true goal in life or his true self. De Bernières also considers the possibility of the hero's failure during his mission and the possibility of self-accomplishment only after the return to the homeland.

At times when the hero's journey is understood as a paradigm for the individual's psychic and spiritual growth, the author reveals a sceptical attitude about individual self-growth. At the same time, the novelist seems to claim that a journey which is performed may not suffice for the individual development, and presents the alternative possibility of the individual's self-growth without any journey to be performed. Louis de Bernières also tries to redefine monomyth in terms of gender and by this opportunity he invites his reader to a reflection upon heroic action which is performed both on the battlefield and in the domestic environment.

In the following, a closer attention given to the characters would better reveal these aspects.

2.3.1 Mandras

One hypostasis or face of the hero, which seems to be the closest to the model of the monomyth of the hero and the quest, is revealed by the character Mandras, a young fisherman from the island of Cephallonia. Although we are not given many details about his origin or birth, as we are not given any particularities about his childhood, he makes his great entrance into the events of the novel in an episode in which the entire village has gathered in order to watch the spectacle of a firing gun.

Mandras is now captured in the status of a naïve and innocent young man willing to explore the unknown and being extremely attracted by guns, gunpowder, and the implied heroic ability of using them. In his absorption by the display of projectiles, he is unable to avoid a ricochet: he is wounded and taken to the doctor's house to be treated. The dignity of our hero seems to be at test when he is carried to the doctor's house in the arms of the village's giant Velisarios and also when he is held down by the same man while being attended by the doctor. These events appear to be an offence against our hero's honour, as he could have walked to the doctor's house by himself and could have endured alone the pain caused by the wound. Being tended by others places Mandras into a childlike hypostasis which exposes his vulnerable and unprotected side and damages his self-inflicted heroic allure.

The humiliation caused by the wound would last longer, but the presence of Pelagia, the doctor's daughter, makes Mandras "aware of his destiny". Unlike the traditional monomyth heroes whose "encounter with the goddess" takes place after the separation from home, Mandras meets his goddess quite early in his experience, suggesting the beginning of his social and sexual maturity. The author has subverted the parameters of the monomyth not only by this premature encounter with the goddess, but also by the inversion of the hierarchies between these two.

The monomythic hero frequently proves his worth and manliness by rescuing a princess, but de Bernières' character is often helped by Pelagia on various, even ridiculous, occasions, as when he is accidentally wounded or when he falls down from a tree upon a garden pot, leaving some crumbs and fragments of terracotta on his backside. Acknowledging his inferiority in relation to Pelagia, Mandras feels the demand of stepping out from his familiar environment into an unknown zone, hoping thus to assert both his private and public value. In his naivety, he claims:

> I love Pelagia, but I know that I will never be a man until I've done something important, something great, something I can live with, something to be esteemed.

That's why I hope there's going to be a war. I don't want bloodshed and glory, I want something to get to grips with. No man is a man until he has been a soldier. (De Bernières, 1995, p. 80)

His willingness to depart from home is stimulated by Dr Iannis, Pelagia's father, who constantly calls him "fool" or "idiot", and also by his patriotic eagerness which reveals a young man's enthusiasm of being useful to his community. Unlike some epic heroes, Mandras is not reluctant to join the war. On the contrary, he says:

I want my call-up immediately. (…) I'm going to make [Pelagia] understand that in defending Greece I will be defending her and every woman like her. It's a question of national salvation. Everyone has the duty to do his utmost. And if I die, then it's too bad, I won't have died for nothing. I will die with the name of Pelagia and the name of Greece equally on my lips, because it amounts to the same thing, the same sacred thing. And if I live, I'll walk with my head held high for the rest of my life, and I'll come back to my dolphins and my nets, and everyone will say, 'That's Mandras, who fought in the war. We owe everything to people like him,' and not Pelagia, and not her father, will be able to look at me and call me a fool and an idiot, and I'll always be more than a nobody-fisherman with terracotta shards in his arse. (De Bernières, 1995, pp. 82–83)

In his frustration induced by the sense of inferiority, Mandras thinks that being a fisherman is not noble enough to make Pelagia, her father, and the entire community respect him. A fisherman's life implies too little work of a heroic nature. In his naivety, Mandras thinks that a war would help him overcome this complex of inferiority and increase his worth.

At the same time, a war would facilitate the fulfilment of one particular thread of fantasy, which is his dream of excelling, the secret desire of becoming a demigod. In other words, Mandras reveals the heroic fantasy of every child: to perform some glorious deeds and, consequently, to be admired by everyone. He is not aware that Pelagia already sees him as a god, like an ancient sculpture, "so beautiful, luminous, and young; Mandras, as exquisite as Apollo" (De Bernières, 1995, p. 99). At this moment, Mandras is confronted with a stringent problem: although he is a man, and a man is presumably in power everywhere, he does not feel himself to be powerful enough.

Michael Kimmel explains that "men often feel themselves to be (…) constrained by a system of stereotypic conventions that leave them unable to live the lives to which they believe they are entitled" (Kimmel, 2000, p. 93). Mandras sets off in pursuit of the warrior's glory, a glory which, according to him, will make him feel powerful, in control of all things, a glory which will also outlive his life.

Very soon in his journey, Mandras faces the display of power. Being powerful seems essential for his transformation and necessary to exceed the fragmented sense of the self that raises self-doubt. As many young people of his age, Mandras has been lured by the heroic aspect of war, imagining that the war will transform men into heroes – immortal men or supermen like Achilles, Odysseus, and Agamemnon – who would be eventually worshiped as such. Much in the line of Odysseus leaving Ithaca for joining the Trojan War and leaving Penelope waiting for his homecoming, Mandras leaves Pelagia who is supposed to wait for him returning gloriously from the war.

Early in his enterprise is he to learn that the power is not to be in possession by individuals. It is the property of a group and it continues to exist only as long as the group exists. The first knowledge that he attains during his journey is that no matter how much he strives to feel powerful at the individual level, he will eventually, in spite of his clear autonomy and unquestionable heroism, be subjected by the group power that emerges and exists independently of his control.

Mandras must also learn the meaning of war, which is beyond the illusion of heroism. If at first war signifies fighting heroically for glory, later it comes to represent a source of immense suffering. The war depicts soldiers on both sides as seeing it to be wretched, dreadful, and bitter. The war is not frightful to them in terms of fighting, since the forces of both sides fight bravely for their cause. The war is dreadful to them because they discovery that they are simple objects of warfare, instruments of a fighting machine, indispensable in an artistic scenario created by a god/leader that uses them for the satisfaction of personal ego.

The soldiers on both sides are abandoned by their supreme powers to starve and freeze in the most ignoble manner. They fight mechanically an enemy which they cannot even hate because their enemies suffer the same disgrace. They are not able to hate anything except the terrible cold they must endure when they are left without proper clothes, food, and medical care. They meet "white death" without honour, death being mostly a kind of relief from this immeasurable suffering, a kind of end for their agonies. Those who survive are doomed to witness the decomposition of their young and strong bodies inflicted by both wounds and cold. Dirty and negligently looking, they become identical, brothers in suffering, aware of their decay and living with the feeling that their bodies do not belong to them any longer. The war is depicted in infernal colours with the cries and shrieks of pain and agony of the already dead as well as of the living dead.

Mandras, in his quest for perpetual glory, honour and esteem, experiences an epiphany: the war is nothing else than Hell. As a typical monomythic hero, Mandras performs his descent into the underworld from which he emerges tremendously transformed. Like Aeneas, who goes to the underworld and meets his father who foretells the hero's future life, Mandras extracts his knowledge from a similar experience. But, unlike Aeneas who is destined for a glorious future, Mandras sees his future as an everlasting ice, a perpetuation of Hell, which is to be experienced throughout his entire life. As he explains,

> the ice screams. It shrieks. And voices call to you out of it. And you look into it and you see people. (…) I saw my father, my father who died, and he was stuck under the ice, and his eyes were staring at me, and his mouth was open, and I hacked with my bayonet. To get him out. And when I got him out it was someone else. I don't know who it was, the ice deceived me, you see. I know I'll never be worm, never. (De Bernières, 1995, p. 155)

It is in this descent into the underworld that Mandras attempts to achieve the "atonement with the father" in the sense of finding his own place in the universe. Instead, however, he fails to understand his mission in life. Fighting bravely together with his Greek comrades to achieve victory over the Italian invaders and restore the much desired harmony of his land, and defeating the enemy at a great cost, Mandras together with his companions would end up themselves as defeated and under enemy control through Hitler's intervention. He discovers that a man cannot attain victory or harmony for his world in the much desired heroic fashion and that a war is manipulated ignobly by a superior force from above.

Mandras also realizes that all soldiers killed in the war have had a meaningless death and that all those who managed to survive in this absurd war will never be able to find a meaning in their existence. Acknowledging the absurdity of war, Mandras cannot commit himself to achieve anything meaningful. His entire existence seems to be reduced to cold and ice, symbolically referring to a life in death, where the individual fails to discover the Self and experiences instead a perpetual emptiness produced and maintained by personal and communal meaningless existence.

Mandras returns home greatly transformed, as most monomythic heroes do, his transformation being threefold: physical, moral, and psychological.

First, his physical transformation is shocking. From a young, well-built and extremely attractive young man, Mandras becomes a kind of "wild man of the ice", a stranger wearing some indefinable, ragged remains of clothes and a cloak of animal skins, and

> in place of shoes his feet were bound with bandages that were both caked with old, congealed blood, and the bright strains of fresh. He was breathing stertorously, and the smell was inconceivably foul; it was the reek of rotting flesh, of suppurating wounds, of dung and urine, of ancient perspiration, and of fear. (De Bernières, 1995, p. 154)

Mandras looks like a demented hermit with a hair without any form or colour. He goes first to Pelagia's house, to his Penelope who is supposed to wait passionately for his return, but, to his surprise, no one is able to recognize him in his new aspect, except Psipsina, the little marten pet from Pelagia's household. This episode clearly reminds us of the mythical Odysseus' return to Ithaca, when only an old dog recognizes his master after such a long absence.

But, while Odysseus is also recognized by the old servants from his household and proves his identity in a unique and heroic manner by the help of his bow, thus imposing himself as the victorious warrior, king, and husband of Penelope, Mandras is recognized neither by Pelagia nor by Dr Iannis, and not even by his old mother Drosoula. Having no victory to boast about and no magical armour which would confer to him a unique and recognizable status, Mandras is diminished not only physically, but also as an individual.

Looking like a corpse with a face that "was as emaciated as that of the saint in his sarcophagus and looked as hollow-eyed and pale as that of someone recently dead but already cold", the two women, Pelagia and Drosoula, still have difficulty in recognizing him (De Bernières, 1995, p. 162). The washing and treatment of his body with herbs, chemicals and balsams suggest mostly the ritual of embalming a dead before the funeral, or the process of mummification, implying that Mandras has been reduced to the status of a well-preserved, but empty body, attended by his bride and mother.

Second, Mandras emerges transformed psychologically as well. The war, in archetypal terms, provides Mandras with the opportunity of overpowering the shadow, the dark aspect of his personal unconscious, which is necessary in the process of self-growth. The confrontation between the ego and the shadow is essential in the process of self-knowledge. During his journey, Mandras must confront "strange monsters" that threaten him "with their maws", "three headed" creatures which wish to "devour" him, symbolically suggesting the confrontation against the complexes of his personal unconscious that prevent his growth. His complex of inferiority, his insecurity concerning his self-worth, as well as his incapacity to attain prestige, glory and esteem during the war function as obstacles for the personal unconscious which thwarts his self-actualization.

His "sacred marriage", which takes place during the journey, is also frustrating. If an encounter with the goddess in archetypal experience equals to a kind of bliss attained by the hero, which suggests an elevated or supreme state of blissful consciousness which contrasts much with the efforts of ordinary waking consciousness, in the case of Mandras this situation is far from being perceived as a kind of bliss.

Instead of a delightful young princess or nymph, in his journey Mandras meets an old hag. Her physical description is conveyed as in the following: "She was small and withered, and she had tied her few strands of hair behind her head. Her back was bowed and bent, her dress was in tatters, and her cheeks were hollow, her chin sharpened, because there was not one tooth in her head" (De Bernières, 1995, p. 172). Her name is Circe, like that of the mythical sorceress, but unlike the mythical nymph who is extremely attractive, this Circe is one-eyed, with a terrible voice resembling the croak of a raven, and Mandras is repelled and horrified by her appearance.

This episode contrasts greatly with the one found in the ancient epic *Odyssey*, in which the nymph transforms Odysseus' men into swines and wishes to do the same with the hero, but the sorceress fails due to Odysseus' quick perception, this victory symbolizing the hero's superior state of blissful consciousness. In the case of de Bernières' hero, Circe feeds him on pigmeat; moreover, she even manages to lure him to bed. Mandras' inability to recognize the trick with the pigmeat and the sexual deceit represents his failure to attain self-completion. The sexual knowledge, which many heroes come to learn as a result of their encounter with goddesses or nymphs, proves their manliness and contributes to their self-growth. Mandras becomes pathetic when he discovers next to him an old hag and when he realizes that he has lost his virginity "to an antique, loveless, solitary crone" (De Bernières, 1995, p. 173).

The essential characteristic of the encounter with the goddess refers to the integration of all the archetypes of the unconscious and the power and wisdom necessary to prevail over the complexes of the personal unconscious, thus providing the possibility of self-accomplishment. For Mandras, this "sacred marriage" represents his failure; he is not strong enough to resist the temptation; he is not wise enough to detect treachery; and he does not experience any sense of beauty that would contribute to his bliss which is necessary for the integration and attainment of a coherent sense of identity. Instead of proving his maleness and masculinity, he grows more insecure than ever. Instead of experiencing an elevating bliss, Mandras degenerates greatly.

Third, Mandras experiences a moral deterioration as well. From the innocent young man playing joyfully with the dolphins like a god, he follows his beautiful patriotic ideals just to discover eventually that these ideals have no validity in this world, that heroism is futile, and that the human existence is meaningless. Mandras becomes dehumanized; in his journey he is surrounded by bears, wild dogs, and wolves, gradually feeding himself like a wild beast, tearing the raw flesh off the abandoned prey with his teeth, and capable of fighting with an eagle for a pigeon. He seems to accommodate himself to this life, thus attaining an animalized perception of existence. Mandras behaves as if he has evacuated his humanness completely in this new awareness of existence, growing indifferent to everything and everyone. He is callous and cold when he leaves the old woman who fell in love with him:

> She tried to stop me leaving, kneeling at my feet and weeping and howling as she clutched my knees. It was pitiful, but I remember thinking that since nothing mattered any more, it did not matter if she too shared in this suffering that has taken the world by storm and laid it all to waste. (De Bernières, 1995, p. 173)

Perceiving the world as meaningless, he imagines that he is blameless and could not be held morally responsible for any cruel or heartless act he would ever commit.

He returns home, greatly transformed, attaining the ultimate knowledge for the human existence, which is that of death, without the opportunity of rebirth. Unable to accomplish the discovery of the self and the prospect of rebirth being shunned, Mandras fails to achieve the psychic wholeness that he sought during his quest.

Concerning the moral and especially the psychological transformation, the monomythic journey represents symbolically a process in which the individual advances from a fragmented sense of identity to an integrated identity with a certain sense of meaning in life. In this respect, it is worth noting the contribution of Jean Bolen who presents this process of individuation in terms of psychological curing of the damage produced by such disorders as multiple personality or psychological dismemberment:

> With the help of the inner self helper in psychotherapy [an archetypal encounter], the many fragmentary personalities become aware of the others, after which they can voluntarily integrate into one personality. To a lesser extent, because the damage done is less (…) [t]he task is not to knit together separate personalities, but to reconnect with cut-off parts of ourselves. Psychological "dis-memberment" takes place in the first half of life (…). To heal and make the whole takes "re-membering". To do this, we must go downward or inward to find the pieces and bring them back to light. (Bolen 1989, p. 291)

In the course of his journey, Mandras fails to attain an integrated identity or a sense of purpose in life. Instead, his fragmented identity grows sharper, leading him to experience a sense of disorder which prevents the development of his innate potentials.

Therefore, he feels the stringent urge to be healed from this psychological chaos, and for this he must "reconnect" with the cut-off parts of himself, to "re-member" the pieces of his own self and attempt to bring them back to light. In order to cure himself, he must integrate his personal consciousness with the unconscious elements of his psyche, and by this to attain a coherent sense of the self.

In order to give himself a chance, Mandras' return to his origin, his homeland, becomes compulsory, and he must remember what he has left there. But his return home is not easy. He must re-encounter his anima, the Mother archetype which is essential for his individual development. Michael Gurian explains that the relation of a male to his mother is fundamental as a result of the archetypal relationship with her: "As we grew up in her arms and in her castle, our mother was, in archetypal terms, like a great nurturing Goddess – the Mother-Creator, the Sacred Queen, the wise Crone and the beautiful Maiden all in one. (…) We were attached to our mothers (or other primary caregivers) in a unique way" (Gurian, 1994, pp. 50–51).

Mandras associates his anima with Pelagia, the young woman from his island, whom he considers to be sacred, an icon, more valuable than the Virgin Queen, the embodiment of beauty and bliss, superior to him, and, therefore, exerting power and authority upon him. It is for her sake that he took off to war, in her name he was planning to achieve prestige and glory.

That is why in his present state the re-encounter with her is extremely difficult and humiliating. Beside the awareness of the complexes and frustrations attained by him during his journey, his return reinforces his sense of inferiority as well as the insecurity in his relation to Pelagia. Any individual willing to become integrated and to attain a psychic wholeness should experience the Mother's unconditional love. In order to achieve the psychological wholeness, the individual must enjoy an unshakable, adamant sense of being loved. The necessity of attaining the wholeness through the mother's love is explained pertinently by the psychologist R. D. Laing in the following:

> Everyone should be able to look back in their memory and be sure he had a mother who loved him, all of him; even his piss and shit. He should be sure his mother loved him just for being himself; not for what he could do. Otherwise he feels he has no right to exist. He feels he should never have been born.
>
> No matter what happens to this person in life, no matter how much he gets hurt, he can always look back to this and feel that he is lovable. He can love himself and he cannot be broken.
>
> You can only be broken if you are already in pieces. As long as my baby-self has never been loved then I was in pieces. By loving me as a baby, you made me whole. (Laing, 1979, p. 172)

Mandras suffers from what R. D. Laing considers to be the state of "chaotic nonentity", which is an extreme version of individual discord. Mandras feels a compelling urge to go to Pelagia's house, make her see him in his deplorable situation and become sure that she can accept and love him in any hypostases the life would expose him. This is the kind of healing that he needs mostly. The wounds on his body are awful, but his inner wounds are even more terrifying. That is why, while being cured by Pelagia's herbs and unguents, he mostly seeks a balm for his soul and his psyche, which could be provided only by his sense of Pelagia's unconditional love for him.

Of course, he still keeps Pelagia's letters which he received while at war as a token of her love for him, but he could not feel the confidence provided by love, since he could not read them. He did not want anybody to read these letters to him, because he considered them as sacred. He did not want anybody to profane his love, and he waited for such a long time for Pelagia to read them to him, which would make him attain a supreme bliss at last. But in order to experience it, he must divulge to her one more weakness – his incapacity to read. This one makes Mandras even more vulnerable and embarrassed, increasing his complex of inferiority, as well as his insecurity concerning his self-worth, especially when Pelagia, a simple woman from his village can read and write, is fluent in Italian and Katharevousa, can read poetry, and, above all, can heal.

In his state of "chaotic non-entity", Mandras gets confused about the feelings of love and hatred. He does not know whether Pelagia or even his mother love or despise him, nor is he sure about his own feelings for them. As a result of his psychological discord, he regresses into a kind of infancy, driving himself into a condition of complete dependency:

> He had been fed with soup poured down a tube into his gullet, and he had neither urinated nor defecated for days until the very time that Drosoula stopped trying to make him do it. Then he had soiled the sheets so copiously that she had to run outside and gag in the street. (De Bernières, 1995, pp. 180–181)

Mandras wants to be certain that both Pelagia and his mother love him unconditionally, no matter how low he would regress. At the same time, in this self-inflicted infancy, he can enjoy the complete attention from both Pelagia and his mother by being nourished, protected and cherished, feeling safe and comforted in their company. Mandras' regress may symbolize his unconscious desire of returning to the maternal womb, which in psychoanalytic terms refers to a paradisiacal state, a place of fulfilled presence, a different universe, closed in and isolated from the world's cruelty and meaninglessness, where an individual feels safe in relation to the outer world.

From a psychoanalytical perspective, this situation provides the possibility of linking the conscious ego and its unconscious counterpart as a necessary prelude to the psychological and spiritual rebirth of an individual, as well as to the development of a personality similar to the archetypal model of a fertility ritual. In archetypal terms, this union with mother may have the purpose of awakening the dormant transformative energy of the Mother archetype for the good of the individual. In other words, Mandras' regress into infancy may suggest his reliance on the transformative energy of mother, which, after a period of gestation, provides the possibility of regeneration or rebirth so desperately needed by him in order to attain a sense of the self.

At the same time, his other fragmentary personality hates both Pelagia and his mother, manoeuvring himself into insanity just for the sake of vengeance or punishment. Thus, although his body is almost completely healed, he refuses to participate in his recuperating process, deliberately torturing Pelagia and his mother, wishing to see them always desperately worried, driving them into a state of continuous despair. Thinking that nobody wants him, Mandras attempts to inflict upon everyone around the same sense of terror, fear and anguish similar to the one that he has experienced throughout his journey and after it.

The situation becomes sinister when, in his present moral decay, he starts abusing Pelagia's feelings, forcing her to read continuously the letters that she sent to him while at war. Although he is aware that her passion for him has ceased, he insists on her reading of the fragments which reveal her feelings at that time, emotionally harming her, reducing her to an extreme and anxious state of embarrassment:

> She felt her cheeks flush with irritation, she was aghast at these geysers of emotion that seemed to be those of another, lesser self. She cringed in the same way as she did when her aunt reminded her of something winsome that she had done or said as a child. The loving words now struck in her throat and left a taste of bitterness on her tongue, but every time that she paused, Mandras would glare at her, his eyes flashing, and would demand that she continue. (De Bernières, 1995, p. 185)

It seems that he wants to impose all the outrageous experiences that he has lived throughout his life upon the ones whom he once has loved, and he wants to inflict as much suffering upon them as he has once experienced. Above all, Mandras has the feeling that no one does love him and people do not want him in their lives, a feeling that makes him evacuate all sensitivity and humaneness out of himself. With a sense of psychological marginalization, he cannot feel integrated into a civilized identity.

While most of the monomythic heroes return home in order to share the achieved gifts with their community, teaching as prophets the ultimate truth, Mandras reveals to his community the only truth that he has learnt during his journey: the monstrosity of human existence. He has grown himself into a monster, causing pain and suffering to people that he once loved, and being incapable of feeling pity or compassion for others. The monstrosity is the state of consciousness that he has achieved in the course of his journey of self-discovery.

The emergence of this new Mandras resembles the psychological process that leads to the division of the consciousness into two opposing psyches of an individual: the good one and the evil one. Carl Jung considers that this phenomenon is deeply fixed in the collective unconscious which functions as the basis upon which the consciousness of the individual develops. Since the collective unconscious is composed of both good and evil aspects, the human being, in the process of development of his individual psyche, assimilates those aspects of the collective unconscious that mostly function in his society.

Therefore, although good and benevolent at the beginning of his self-discovery process, Mandras assimilates mostly the malign aspects of his world, which eventually lead to the development of his individual psyche as controlled by an evil and destructive consciousness. The psychoanalyst Erik Erikson sees this process of self-individuation in the following terms:

> Identity formation normatively has its dark and negative side, which throughout life can remain an unruly part of the total identity. Every person and every group harbours a *negative identity* as the sum of all those identifications and identity fragments which the individual had to submerge in himself as undesirable or irreconcilable or which his group has [been] taught to perceive as the mark of fatal "difference" in sex role or race, in class or religion. (Erikson, 1975, p. 20)

Consequently, having the evil aspects dominating his psyche and his identity formation, Mandras projects these evil moral categories onto others, causing their suffering.

Nevertheless, although the evil consciousness dominates his psyche, he makes an enormous effort to suppress the negative aspects of his personal unconscious. He struggles to bring to light the positive aspects that may come to dominate his psyche and determine his sense of purpose and identity. Mandras' psychological struggle resembles the individual's confrontation with his own shadow in his willingness to establish his personal identity. As Jung explains,

> the shadow is a moral problem that changes the whole ego-personality, for no one can become conscious of the shadow without considerable moral effort. To become conscious of it involves recognizing the dark aspects of the personality as present and real. This act is the essential condition for any kind of self-knowledge, and it therefore, as a rule, meets with considerable resistance. (Jung, 1971, p. 145)

Mandras grows more and more aware of the damaging dark aspects of his personality and is willing to change. However, the slaying of his inner dragons is not an easy task. They have rooted themselves too deeply into Mandras' mind and soul. In order to kill these monsters, Mandras should die as well, since only death can defeat them and restore Mandras' psychological and spiritual goodness.

In a symbolical manner alluding to the Christian myth of Jesus' resurrection, Mandras has laid in bed motionless, as if in a tomb, from the Holy Thursday before the great celebration of Easter till Saturday night, when he gets up, dressed in black, takes a candle and joins the processions of icons to the monastery. When the priest appears with his lighted candle and exclaims "Christos anesti", Pelagia and Drosoula wonder: "Mandras anesti? Is Mandras risen?" (De Bernières, 1995, p. 182). Mandras' resurrection is promising, especially when "Mandras seemed to be his old self" (De Bernières, 1995, p. 183), but the illusion of his salvation lasts too short, for on Sunday evening he returns to his bed, this time not just simulating death, but living death in "the most extreme spiritual pain".

This experience could be considered as Mandras' second descent into the underworld. Here, like Dante's characters of *Inferno* who suffer terrible spiritual pain after their death, Mandras cannot attain redemption since his sense of guilt is great. When death cannot provide an end to his pain and suffering, and resurrection fails to cure Mandras, he continues to exist in his own Hell created by his sense of guilt and need for self-punishment.

Mandras' underworld is a place of torment, suffering and guilt. Ironically, the salvation from this infernal anxiety is brought by the foreign invasion. In an absurd and bizarre manner, what neither death nor resurrection could convey is provided by the invasion which brings not only relief, but creates a purpose in Mandras' otherwise meaningless existence.

It is exactly this purpose in life that alleviates Mandras' existence, since he can, finally, become useful to something and feel himself valuable. This prospect of becoming worthy animates him to such an extent that he climbs out of his bed completely cured and goes to the sea, swimming with his dolphins in a harmonious way as if he has never been away, returning "refreshed, the salt water drying in his tousled hair, a smile upon his face, his muscles in his torso uncontracted" (De Bernières, 1995, p. 212).

His union with the sea symbolically suggests the necessity of integration of his personal consciousness with the unconscious elements of his psyche, which may endow, eventually, with a coherent sense of the self. The juxtaposition of the images of fire and water suggests the coming together of opposites, which join life and death, conscious and unconscious, ideal and real. Mandras' metamorphosis by the power of fire and water hints to the myth of alchemical transformation, which Jung considers as a metaphor for the process of self-individuation.

In order to be completed, the alchemical transformation needs an essential element, so that a base metal would be changed into silver or gold. Mandras' transformation from an ordinary to a valuable status should be provided by separation, the essential ingredient in his completion process. Therefore, he should perform a journey once again, in hope of attaining his true goal in life, of detaching himself from his negative aspects and of discovering, finally, his true self.

In the monomythic experience, the hero is helped by a guide to overcome the fragmented sense of identity, a sense that stimulates the rise of self-doubt. Mandras is desperate to succeed this time, and, like a monomythic hero, he needs the support of a tutor who will lead him wisely throughout his journey. His mentor becomes Hector, a perverted image of the mythical Hector, who teaches Mandras not just the method of slaying monsters, but also teaches him the secret of letters and reading, as well as the meaning of life.

Mandras' initiation takes place when he proves his manliness and worth by beating to death an old man, who, according to Hector, is a "dirty old thief". Under Hector's guidance, Mandras learns that he must not feel compelled by the need of dealing directly with his own negative characteristics, which are both humiliating and disturbing. Instead, he grows aware that these negative aspects can be projected onto others, a discovery which is extremely invigorating for him. He is surprised at seeing that it is more facile to fight with outer monsters rather than with his inner ones:

> It was easier at each stroke. In fact it became exhilaration. It was as if every rage from the earliest year of childhood was welling up inside him, purging him, leaving him renewed and cleansed. The old man, who had been yelping and jumping sideways at every blow, spinning and cowering, finally threw himself to the ground, whining piteously, and Mandras suddenly knew that he could be a god. (De Bernières, 1995, p. 232)

By presuming himself almost a god, Mandras transgresses. Misusing the heroic impulse, he learns the satisfying way of projecting his undesirable characteristics onto others by creating outside monsters that should be slain. He indulges himself into the criminal act, casting all his negative aspects and frustrations upon others, inventing enemies when there are no actual ones:

> the [old] man had been sentenced to death, and was going to die anyway. He looked a little like Dr Iannis, with his thin grey hair and prominent occipital bone. Dr Iannis, who didn't think him worth a dowry. Who cares about one more useless old man? (De Bernières, 1995, p. 233)

It is worth noting what the social psychologist Sam Keen says in this respect: "Depth psychology has presented us with the undeniable wisdom that the enemy is constructed from the denied aspects of the self" (Keen, 1986, p. 11).

As a consequence of his identity crises, following the denial of the aspects of the self, individuals such as Mandras become prey, easily exploited by political leaders; they "become models of a sudden surrender to total doctrines and dogmas in which the negative identity appears to be the desirable and the dominant one" (Erikson, 1975, p. 20).

It is that Mandras now idealizes Hector, worships him as o deity and follows him in his every criminal act. Mandras adopts Hector's enthusiasm in "liberating the masses", burning the Greek villages of "betrayers", killing the "collaborators", and raping their daughters. This kind of "liberation" becomes Mandras' purpose in life, a purpose which he has failed to attain throughout his long journey of self-discovery. Now Mandras can experience the much desired exhilarating bliss, which could be achieved, ironically, only through his outrageous cruelty and display of violence.

The role of the shadow in the formation of his new identity is relevant here, since it permits the rise of a destructive violence which the psychoanalyst Erich Fromm considers as typically human and atypical to any other species in the animal regnum, which, unlike humans, do not possess the mental ability of projecting any moral categories onto others:

> We must distinguish in man *two entirely different kinds of aggression*. The first, which he shares with all animals, is a phylogenetically programmed impulse to attack (or to flee) when vital interests are threatened. This *defensive*, "benign" aggression is in the service of survival of the individual and the species, is biologically adaptive, and ceases when the threat has ceased to exist. The other type, "malignant" aggression, i.e., destructiveness and cruelty, is specific to the human species and virtually absent in most mammals; it is not phylogenetically programmed and not biologically adaptive; it has no purpose, and its satisfaction is lustful. (Fromm, 1973, p. 4)

Mandras, under the guidance of his mentor Hector, develops this type of malignant aggression, which is displayed only for the sake of his personal satisfaction, an indulgence which derives from his capacity of overpowering someone and which strengthens his illusion of self-confidence. The intensification of his self-esteem is also provided by his newly acquired skill of reading, a skill gained also under Hector's supervision. Mandras takes great pleasure in his reading classes; he has the impression of being initiated into a sacred knowledge, to which only the chosen ones have access. He experiences a kind of ecstasy not only for being initiated into the secret meaning of letters, but also for being illuminated by the great discovery of the book entitled *What Is to Be Done*.

This book seems to be a revelation to our hero, who emerges transformed once again after such an experience. The role of icon that has been held by Pelagia's letters is now replaced by this book, which apparently emancipates him and enlightens his horizons by the theories of Marx, Engels, Plekhanov, and Lenin, and provides a new and unique opportunity in his life:

> He might hold [the book] in his hands as though it were printed upon sheets of diamond. At night he might kiss its covers and sleep with it beneath his head, as though its inconceivable wisdom might seep by capillary action into his brain. One day he would be an intellectual, and neither the doctor nor Pelagia would ever be able to say otherwise. He imagined himself as a schoolteacher, with everyone calling him 'daskale' and listening avidly to his opinions in the kapheneion. He imagined himself as the mayor of Lixouri. (De Bernières, 1995, pp. 282–283)

This transformation is essential, since it reveals that Mandras' awareness of this world's values changes. From the aspirations in a world based on warrior ethos ideals, Mandras acknowledges some other values, which are now of intellectual and political nature, and which, once achieved, may be satisfactory as well. The transformation thrusts Mandras into an elevated state of powerful blissful consciousness, never experienced by him before, which is a state that stimulates completely his vital energy.

Mandras resembles here the monomythic hero who has reached a nirvanic experience and indulges himself into this experience by refusing to leave it, and, as a typical monomythic hero, Mandras should feel compelled to return to the natural waking consciousness that invests him with power and provides a purpose to the self. But, unlike the paradigmatic hero, de Bernières' character is not yet aware that this blissful conscience is gained at the expense of some corrupted ideals that have completely dehumanized him.

Louis de Bernières has inverted some units of myth, as when Mandras, in a typical heroic manner, performs a journey and a quest, and emerges completely transformed especially by his newly acquired ability of reading, but, ironically, instead of achieving the expected spiritual growth or harmony, he emerges as a degraded individual with a perverted sense of the self, a rapist whose prior ideals have been completely corrupted by the totalitarian mirages.

Following the trajectory of some successive transformations through a certain number of mythemes or units of myths, de Bernières plays with the expectations of the reader by reversing such mythemes as dissension and ascension. Each time the character dissents to the realm of death, one expects him to grow elevated by such an experience, to get the knowledge that will strengthen his self-awareness and, eventually, provide him with the pathway into a sacred or mystical realm.

Instead, Mandras decays physically, spiritually and morally with each descent. The repetition of the same motif fortifies the impression of the transgression to the extent of losing any hope in a possible rise.

A similar situation occurs in the case of ascension. The most striking examples of Mandras' ascent are the ones referring to Mandras' symbolical resurrection during the Easter celebration and his elevation into a nirvanic experience. The two examples offer the expectation of the protagonist's psychological and spiritual rise. Instead, Mandras' rise and enlightenment lead to a completely perverted manipulation of reality, preventing any possible ascension.

It is now that he becomes mostly dangerous, "full of his purported glory and his new ideas, expectant of the dutiful and admiring attention of the fiancée that he had not seen for years, and intent upon exacting his revenge" (De Bernières, 1995, p. 446). Since it is Mandras' second coming, the novelist plays with the reader's expectation based on the motif of remembering one's previous identity. When revealed in other literary works, this motif corresponds to the recovery of a lost kingdom or the remembering of one's divine lineage, a situation that proves an integrated and asserted self, confident in his life's purpose.

Mandras lives in the illusion of the asserted self, illusion which empowers him to feel in control of everything. The false impression about his empowered self, gained either through fear, lack of confidence or lust for power, leads him to forget his true self-identity, and he becomes unrecognizable. De Bernières begins the representation of recognition motif by the description of Mandras' physical transformation:

> A man came in that [Pelagia] did not recognize, except that he looked very like Drosoula had done before the war. There was the same distended belly and thighs, the same round, coarse face, the identical heavy eyebrows and thickened lips. Three years of living in idleness upon the bounty of the bounty of the British and the booty stolen from peasants had turned the handsome fisherman into nothing if not a toad. (…) She (…) looked at those gross and transfigured features, and felt a pang of horror. (De Bernières, 1995, p. 446)

The novelist builds this situation upon the mythical reference to ancestral lineage, relying heavily on the formidable aspect of Drosoula before the war. At the same time, Louis de Bernières inverts the symbolical implication of this situation while referring to Mandras' transformation into a toad. If his mother's physical aspect ever horrified anyone, still everybody respected this woman for her moral integrity. Mandras' transformation into a toad, however, with its symbolical reference to dishonesty and fraudulence, denies any possibility of decency and righteousness.

The novelist proves playful in relying on the fairy tale motif of transformation of a prince into a frog, where the second transformation is provided from frog to prince as a result of moral integrity and the great capacity to love. No such transformation is to be expected from Mandras.

At the same time, Mandras' physical transformation is presented as resulting from his moral depravity. Similar to Dante's Lucifer – who was once one of the most beautiful angels of God but as a result of his moral transgression becomes an ugly parody of Holy Trinity and is thrown into the last circle of Inferno – Mandras' initial Divine Beauty also turns to ugliness. The great mystery of evil is to pervert everything which is beautiful when the hero lacks a strong system of values.

The British writer prevents this expectation by revealing Mandras' inner distorted morality, as well as the self-inflicted and perverted image of the self. Instead of becoming a prince, like in fairy tales, Mandras is transformed into an ogre as a result of his inner monstrosity.

The illusion of the asserted self leads him to the desire of power and control over others. In this respect, James Redfield mentions four strategies of repressing an environment for achieving personal power (Redfield, 1997). Intimidation is the first, when one holds control over an environment through threats of exploding into rage and aggression. The second strategy is interrogation, when one holds the control by investigating and criticizing others. Victimization is the third strategy and it refers to the control achieved through uses of sympathy or sense of guilt. The last one is aloofness, when one holds control through the use of silence and ambiguity.

These are also the strategies which are employed by Mandras in his quest for personal power. Symbolically, Pelagia represents the environment over which he hopes to exert his assumed power and authority. Her being interrogated by him about letters and love, his judging and criticizing of her, the victimization of Pelagia through the exploration of her sense of guilt for loving a fascist captain, his menacing of reference to his possible silence over her adultery with an enemy (indicating to her probable abuse by the "patriots"), and the final intimidation of Pelagia through his attempt to rape her suggest Mandras' manner of imposing his self-inflicted authority. This false impression about his empowered self leads him to a monstrosity with devastating effects for both his community and his own self.

The quest for personal empowerment and assertion leads Mandras to the oblivion of his own identity. The motif of recognizing one's identity is inverted again, because now this motif should be understood as a rediscovery of the lost identity instead of a discovery of a new one. As a consequence of his own monstrosity, the motif of recognition of someone's identity is reshaped by the novelist into the motive of self-knowledge with its consequent implications:

> There was a place, once, where all had sparkled with delight and innocence. He stood still a moment, recalling where it was. He swayed on his feet, nearly fell backwards, and the peasants in their houses looked out and wondered. They did not know him,

although he seemed familiar, and they thought it better not to interfere. (...) They stared at him through their shutters, and watched him lumber past. (De Bernières, 1995, p. 452)

Only by experiencing the highest degree of human transgression could Mandras move toward a profound understanding of his own identity and his purpose of life. The hero's journey signifies a conscious decision of the hero to engage into the journey of self-discovery, which implies the obligatory confrontation of his complexes of the personal unconscious as well as the archetypes of the collective unconscious. The protagonist's awareness of the fact that his journey does not result in the expected rise, his understanding that this journey only corrupts him, and his acceptance of a necessary defeat have an epiphanic function.

At the end of his road, he gains a sort of comprehension of his own nature and his own fallibility. His greatest wisdom is attained at the end of his journey and consists of the awareness that his possible innocence and inner harmony could be achieved only as a fisherman in the realm of the sea.

The fusions of metaphors referring to fishing imagery and piscine symbolism create a powerful conceit, which is a characteristic of density in Louis de Bernières' poetics. Can Mandras be healed by his cathartic revelation or by the waters of the sea? We do not know. But we can hypothesize that the waters of the sea may represent a sacred space, where the mystery of transformation takes place.

Through the symbol of water, the return to the origin is suggested, a return having the purpose of revelation and renewal, and we are entitled to expect that it would heal the schism within the hero's psyche and soul. Mandras' last depiction as naked, while entering the sea, suggests symbolically his complete detachment from all false images of his own self and the final re-encounter with his true self. And if Mandras' journey, per total, could be considered as a complete failure, due to his moral transgression, his final self-discovery is his victory, since he achieves the supreme knowledge that provides his psychic and spiritual wholeness.

If Mandras as a character has the purpose of portraying an aspect of human psyche, we consider that he represents the unconscious. His final union with the water of the sea – a symbol of the unconscious – and with his dolphins, becomes metaphorical, in that his conscious refuses to accept the random chaos of life and accepts only the comforting harmony of the unconscious. This last metaphor suggests also the ultimate mystery of death which transforms the material world of the body into the spiritual world of the psyche. Is this metaphor suggesting the human condition in the postmodern world?

With regard to the monomyth, we can notice that Louis de Bernières revises this experience by incorporating some new stages. Contrary to Campbell's formula which exhibits the end of the journey with the hero's homecoming, de Bernières presents Mandras, whose each end of the journey signifies a beginning of a new one, as being engaged in a journey which is cyclical and thus reiterated for many times.

The reiteration of the hero's journey, a new dimension of the monomyth, happens due to the unstable system of values of our protagonist Mandras, which can be easily shattered by the events of his environment, as a result of fear, insecurity, or as a result of his great aspiration to succeed, to hold power, to be in control of all things. Therefore, in the course of his journey, Mandras fails to consider or ignores completely the earlier established values, changing them with new ones, which are convenient to him at a certain moment of his existence.

Having an imbalanced system of values, Mandras becomes an autocrat, a rapist, a thief. Mandras also fails to recognize his true purpose in life. In this respect, we can consider that it is another of the novelist's subversions of the conventions of the monomyth, because the hero's journey is generally understood as a paradigm for individual' psychic and spiritual growth, but Louis de Bernières presents a rather sceptical attitude about Mandras' self-growth and self-accomplishment.

The novelist suggests that a journey or a number of journeys performed does not suffice for the individual development. The fact that Mandras performs his ultimate journey into the realm of water of his native sea after a final moment of revelation, suggests that an alternative to the motif of journey exists and that an individual can attain the sense of the self without the conventional element of departure.

In Mandras' case, the novelist introduces the element of a final departure which is death, since the character commits suicide by entering the sea, where water symbolically claims the idea of purification, despite his action being sinful from an orthodox perspective.

2.3.2 Captain Antonio Corelli

This character is introduced quite late in the novel and when we first meet him he seems to be a self-sufficient young man. This strategy is employed by Louis de Bernières in his attempt to subvert hero-myth and quest paradigm, an attempt which is necessary for his revising, rewriting, rethinking, and reimagining process of the monomyth of the hero and the quest.

The novelist undermines the well-known pattern of separation-adventure-return by Captain Corelli being placed in the middle of his journey in Cephallonia and as belonging to the occupying troops of Italian soldiers who have just invaded the island. The hypostasis of invader suggests a heroic achievement, which is revealed by an arrogant, *miles gloriosus* type, boastful of his *kleos*.

The novelist, however, subverts the reader's expectations by presenting a hero without any heroic ambition. Still, the reader is told that this is not the result of a shameful lack of courage. On the contrary, when necessary, Captain Corelli displays an impressive courage and heroism, winning battles even unarmed.

Captain Corelli also admires heroes, like all warriors do. It is that his sense of heroism differs from the traditional *arête* standards. His understanding of excellence on the battlefield does not correspond to a warrior's capacity to kill opponents in the combat. To him, the warrior's excellence is redefined when the hero is glorified for saving lives: Corelli expresses great admiration for Carlos, "one of our heroes [who] has a hundred medals for saving life, and none for taking it" (De Bernières, 1995, p. 202).

Corelli's lack of any military ambition stems from his great love of music. He does not seem to be embarrassed at all while admitting his reasons for enrolling in the Army:

> When I joined, Kyria Pelagia, Army life consisted mainly of being paid for sitting about doing nothing. Plenty of time for practice, you see. I had a plan to become the best mandolin player in Italy, and then I would leave the Army and earn a living. I didn't want to be a café player, I wanted to play Hummel and Conforto and Giulianni. There's not much demand, so you have to be very good. (…) It was a plan that went wrong; the Duce got some big ideas. (De Bernières, 1995, p. 206)

Moreover, his preference to be called "Maestro" instead of "Captain" indicates the superiority of music over any military ambition in his identity formation.

A man, who would dare to mock everything soldierly, displays, nevertheless, soldierly discipline when it comes to music, even if it is being performed in most bizarre circumstances:

> His battery had a latrine known as 'La Scala' because he had a little opera club that shat together there at the same time every morning, sitting in a row on the wooden plank with their trousers about their ankles. He had two baritones, three tenors, a bass, and a counter-tenor who was much mocked on the account of having to sing all the women's parts, and the idea was that each man should expel either a turd or a fart during the crescendos, when they could not be heard above the singing. In this way the indignity of communal defecation was minimized, and the whole encampment would begin the day humming a rousing tune that they had heard wafting out of the heads. (De Bernières, 1995, p. 193)

This lowly, bizarre and obscene depiction of the opera club as opposed to the sublime feeling produced by music seems to create a metaphor of human condition. Relying on the intertextual relations referring to the ancient concept of the music of spheres existent in a divinely ordered universe, as well as the pleasure that the music offers, the novelist tries to emphasize that this is the only possible harmony to be achieved on a chaotic land. The opposition between the sublime and the ridiculous is contracted into an imagery that induces a cathartic experience, necessary to heal the horrors endured by humans during the war.

In the course of human history, music has been perceived as having some dualistic aspects. Nietzsche's famous distinction between Dionysian art and the art of Apollo is noteworthy in this respect: the former has been considered as intoxicating and orgasmic, whereas the latter as calm, reflective, ordered, and balanced. Corelli's use of music in a quasi-ritualistic manner, although revealed in the most ignoble mode in the latrines, refers to the act of catharsis as an attempt of purgation of evil emotions, which is essential for the purification of the community that would lead, eventually, to the establishment of order and harmony.

Corelli's attitude towards Wagner's music can be associated with the struggle between Apollonian and Dionysian forces. Michael Bell mentions that in "German post-romantic tradition through Schopenhauer, Wagner, [and] Nietzsche (…) music expressed a pre-verbal realm of feeling. It was associated with the primordial state which may engulf civilized and rational order" (Bell, 1997, p. 76).

The Apollonian Corelli, representing light, balance and order, could neither accept nor promote Wagner's music which is associated with elevation of individuality to the level of absolute, because its ecstatic and frenetic character leads to the creation of an ideology of superman, related to Hitler and his heroic code.

What kind of quest does Corelli perform then? If it is not based on heroic fulfilment, we would incline to suggest that his journey represents an archetypal quest of an artist in his attempt to give a material form to his revelations. And as with other archetypal heroes performing a quest, Corelli must slay dragons, that is to say, all the "negative" aspects of his personality which are generally hidden in the human psyche.

Corelli's confrontation with the shadow takes place through music, since it provides a more effortless access to the personal unconscious. His evil aspects are revealed by his appartenance to the fascist army, which is symbolically associated with intoxication, disorder and chaos. His recognition of the dark aspects of his personality is exposed by the way in which he makes jokes about himself; also, despite being a fascist soldier, the recognition is revealed by his refusal to accept Wagner as an exponent of proto-fascist ideology, as well as by his dishonourable manner of exposing the fascist uniform. The last aspect is presented in the most hilarious manner through the eyes of Carlos:

> I noticed an appalling and very rank stench, but I went in, only to see a raw of soldiers shitting at their perches, red in the face, singing at full heart, hammering at their steel helmets with spoons. I was both confused and amazed, especially when I saw that there was an officer sitting there amongst the men, insouciantly conducting the concert with the aid of a feather in his right hand. Generally one salutes an officer in uniform, especially when he is wearing his cap. (…) I did not know the regulation that governs the saluting of an officer in uniform who has his breeches at half-mast during a drill that consists of choral elimination in occupied territory. (De Bernières, 1995, p. 193)

Corelli's resistance to the seductive emotional appeal of Wagner's music, with its implicit ideology, to which other characters succumb, reveals his control over the temptations of the shadow that leads to his self-growth. Symbolically, his holding of control over the powers of the shadow in the "musical form" suggests his capacity of bringing the calm, ordered and balanced atmosphere to his environment. Dealing with the undesirable characteristics of his personality, Corelli acquires the ability to discover, as Jung says, "a deeper source of [one's] spiritual life", which is essential for his quest.

The confrontation of the archetypal shadow, which represents a phase of internal transformation, prepares the quest-hero to engage into the trial, which is the next essential part of his journey. The new contest – the encounter with the goddess – is significant for the elevation and self-assurance of the hero.

The Goddess encountered by Corelli during his journey is represented by Pelagia, the doctor's daughter, who, at first, is revealed in the hypostasis of a malign crone and witch struggling for pre-eminence in her battle with Corelli. Pelagia's attempts to make Corelli's life unbearable during his staying in her house – such as placing the pine marten into his bed, or letting him stay hungry and watch her and Dr Iannis eat, and many other humiliations that she imposes upon him – suggest, symbolically, the re-enactment of the primordial times when, as Campbell outlines, the goddesses struggled for supremacy over the divine masculine invaders who wanted to dominate the universe. In an extremely playful manner, the roles of oppressor and oppressed become subverted, which increases the tension in the readers' expectation concerning the dominant patriarch. During their first meetings, Pelagia is represented as an almost fearsome figure having a considerable knowledge of herbs, thinking of poisoning the Captain, and considering even the possibility of shooting him.

At the same time, Pelagia becomes a kind of *femme fatale* for our hero by shattering Corelli's world from within: she becomes the object of his desire, he dreams of her every night, and he is tormented extremely, especially when being forced by circumstances to sleep in her bed alone. The charming temptress Pelagia casts her fatal spell upon Corelli, ensnaring him into her net without allowing any possibility of escape. In archetypal terms, Corelli's being tested by a *femme fatale* may be considered as his struggle against the dangerous sexual and personal alternatives to the real purpose of a quester journey.

Pelagia reveals the destroyer features of the Mother Goddess, but, simultaneously, she possesses, without any doubt, the opposite facet of the Goddess, which is that of the benign, loving and creative Mother who nurtures her universe. The fundamental transformation of the malefic Mother into a harmless and caring consort is achieved through the wisdom and talent of our hero who, symbolically, confronts the possible anxieties of the personal unconscious in his attempt to achieve his psychological wholeness.

Corelli understands the patriarchal domination over the other only in terms of care and love. In this respect, Dalai Lama's words are relevant:

> The more we care for the happiness of others, the greater our own sense of well-being becomes. Cultivating a close, warm-hearted feeling for others automatically puts the mind at ease. This helps remove whatever fears or insecurities we may have and gives us the strength to cope with any obstacles we encounter. It is the ultimate source of success in life. (Dalai Lama, 2010)

The essential function of Corelli's "sacred marriage" refers to the union of all archetypes of the unconscious, when the power and wisdom confront the possible anxieties of the personal unconscious. The character's wisdom is implied by his efforts to go beyond the interests of his ego while cultivating feelings of care and love for others, and these efforts lead him to the accomplishment of an integrated personality. The security provided by the Mother's unconditional love and the capacity of the individual to share this love contribute to the psychological wholeness of the hero.

In the Indian Tantric philosophy, the Mother Goddess is alluded to as the energy of the Mother Goddess Kundalini, where a dormant potential force is lying coiled at the base of each individual spine, waiting for its release which would eventually lead to a sense of enlightenment or bliss signifying the integration of all aspects of one's personality.

One of the most preeminent Indian philosophers of the twentieth century, Sri Aurobindo, refers to Kundalini as "the divine power asleep in the lowest physical centre which awakened in the yoga, ascends in light through the opening centres [in the spine] to meet the Divine in the highest centre and so connect the manifest and the unmanifested, joining spirit and Matter" (Sri Aurobindo, 1996, p. 977).

In our context, this meticulous process of purification and meditation in the Tantric philosophy can be associated with the archetypal journey of the hero. The journey has the purpose of awaking the dormant creative energy of the Mother archetype, which is congenial for both the hero and his community.

Carl Jung claims that the union with the Mother Goddess stimulates a fundamental change in the individual. In the light of both Jungian perspective and that of the Tantric philosophy, Corelli's reunion with the goddess, that is with Pelagia, has a transformative effect upon the hero in that his creative powers become acknowledged and contribute to the attaining of a sense of bliss which is beneficial to him and to his community.

Don Adams, in discussing the pattern of the "quest romance", presents for comparison the metaphor of the poet's quest in which the hero is the poet, the damsel in distress is the poem, and the monster represents the forces impeding the creative process (Adams, 1997, p. 40). The critic develops this metaphor by suggesting that the hero as a poet has to perform two quests: "the quest for sublime and the quest to write a poem *about* the quest for the sublime – what we might call the quest for composition" (Adams, 1997, p. 47).

This assertion can be extended to our hero, Antonio Corelli, a musician who performs his journey in search of the sublime which could be attained through his art. In this respect, it has been frequently noticed the existence of an artistic dyad which appears when an artist, in his creative process, relies upon the dialogue with another precious person who functions for him as an inspirational muse.

Consequently, we consider Pelagia to be Corelli's muse, who inspires him throughout his creative quest. She represents a crucial figure for Corelli, since she embodies the divine powers of the archetypal feminine, absolutely a dual Jungian archetype: anima, which is both creative and destructive. Since anima may be considered as the totality of the unconscious feminine psychological aspects that a male is endowed with, this male could be devastated by this duality. Corelli, at this stage of his development, experiences psychic impoverishment and imbalance, his vulnerability stemming from "being overwhelmed or rendered mentally ill by the unconscious content of his own psyche" (Crone, 2010, p. 128).

Louis de Bernières' hero-artist has to cross this threshold and establish a harmonious incorporation of his male and female sides which represent the conscious and the unconscious, respectively. The artist should generate the union of the opposites representing the dimension of worldly reality and the transcendental dimension of the imagination in order to be able to begin the creative process. Although anima has a devastating effect upon the artist, it is at the same time the source of his creative ability.

Corelli's anima, Pelagia, overwhelms completely our hero-quester, but soon she actually helps him bring to light of the consciousness his latent talent. As we are told in the novel, Corelli got

> captivated by the appealing tranquillity of the sleeping girl, and felt that it would have been a desecration to awake her by clattering abut. (...) He looked down upon her and experienced the urge to crawl in beside her (...) but instead he returned to his room and took Antonia out of her case. He began to practice fingerings with his left hand, sounding the notes minimally by hammering on and pulling off with his fingers rather than using a plectrum. Tiring of this, he took a plectrum and laid the side of his right hand across the bridge so that he could mute the strings and play 'sordo'. It made a sound very like a violin playing pizzicato, and with great concentration he set himself to playing a very difficult and rapid piece by Paganini that consisted entirely of that effect. (De Bernières, 1995, p. 219)

We see in the novel that Corelli reveals the capacity to acknowledge his anima when it manifests itself, and this ability of discerning the anima from reality leads him to his successful artistic self-expression.

As George Hagman considers,

> self-expression in artistic experience is not limited to emotion, affect, or even ideas or impressions (although it may contain all of these). The form of self-expression contained in artistic creation is best captured in the idea of *being*, of conveying in the work aspects of how it feels to *be* the living person whom one is. However, art is not simply a mirror, a representation of ourselves; it is a new creation that evokes self-experience and embodies the self-in-relation through aesthetic perfection. (Hagman, 2005, p. 5)

It is this aesthetic perfection that Corelli is trying to attain through the continuous dialogue between his artistic self and his artwork, a dialogue which is accompanied by perpetual oscillation of states of emotional tension and self-experience. As in the case of most real artists, the sense of concord between the internal and external aspects of an artistic subjectivity is self-affirming and delightful, while its opposite, the discord, inflicts various degrees of self-crisis.

If we consider the artist's artwork symbolically as both beloved and an object of the artistic quest, we may suggest that Pelagia functions as his beloved, his dyad which fuels his desire to create, but, at the same time, she becomes the object of his artistic pursuit, that is, his music. "Pelagia's March", Corelli's artistic masterpiece, results from the union of opposites, from experiencing the aesthetic concord that makes our artist feel invigorated, animated, a feeling that leads him to develop his work of art toward greater perfection. Louis de Bernières presents this creative moment in the following:

Corelli looked at [Pelagia's] silhouette against the light of the window, and the tune came into his head. He could visualize the patterned patrol of his fingers on the fretboard of the mandolin, he could hear the disciplined notes ringing from the treble, singing the praise of Pelagia as they also portrayed her wrath and her resistance. It was a march, a march of a proud woman who prosecuted war with hard words and kindness. He heard three simple chords and a martial melody that implied a world of grace. He heard the melody rise and swell, breaking into a torrent of bright tremolo more limpid than the song of thrushes, more pellucid than the sky. (De Bernières, 1995, p. 291)

The window, with its symbolical suggestion of a mirror that represents reality, refers to any artwork as imitation of reality, but not only, since art is a representation of ourselves; it reflects the self-experience and, at the same time, evokes the self in relation to the outer world. We think that Corelli is inspired by some states of emotional tension and self-experience, such as his love for Pelagia, his admiration for her, and by his idealization of her beauty and character, but his inspiration is also stimulated by the external tension of the outside world – the war – that leaves a mark upon his composition. As Professor R. A. Sharpe suggests,

> music is surrounded not only by texts, dances, dramatic situations, liturgies and narrative programmes but also by associations that may not be merely personal but may form connections with the landscape and history of the composer's native land, with the Zeitgeist and with a social and political context that form an aura, a rich backcloth, in terms of which we "read" the music. (Sharpe, 2004, p. 3)

Returning to the framework of the monomyth, Corelli's quest for the object of his art and the quest for composition may symbolize, in archetypal terms, the conjunction of the opposites, which Jung calls as "mysterium coniunctionis", the fusion of the unconscious and the conscious, fantasy and real. Louis Freiberg, in his study entitled "New Views of Art and the Creative Process in Psychoanalytical Ego Psychology", while elaborating on creativity as an activity of the ego, puts forward the following statement:

> Creation may be characterized psychoanalytically as a process having two phases, inspiration and elaboration. In the first (inspiration), impulses from the Id attained a high degree of expression, but this occurs only under the close control of the ego that receives their powerful manifestations, shuts off the supply when it chooses, and turns them to its own uses. The artist builds upon the partial alteration of the fantasy, which has occurred unconsciously, but at least a significant part of the work is conscious. The impulses, having achieved partial expression, are no longer in the position to exercise control, and the work of art may acquire greater independence from their demands, i.e., secondary autonomy. The elaborative phase of creation follows and it is then that conscious relationships may be established. Connections are made,

patterns are created, and communication is possible. A product emerges which is modified or even transformed into something, which can be received and understood by another person. The material is now subjected to an entirely different set of rules, the requirements of society, of communication, of art. (Freiberg, 1965, pp. 239–240)

According to Ernst Kris, one of the leading ego psychologists, the act of creation relies on the dynamic interchange between conscious and unconscious processes of thought, between illusion and reality. This aspect becomes essential when we consider that a great artistic masterpiece must function under the conditions and terms that are completely opposite to those of the unconscious or dreaming. After all, any object of art subsists in and for the real world.

It is worth mentioning here the contribution of Gilbert J. Rose, who presents the creative act as an explicit psychological process. He considers that every artist attempts to restore the phase of early state of perfection, where the child experiences the sense of being one with the idealized and omnipotent mother. According to Rose, "everyman has undergone separation from what was primordial, unitary pre-self, each of us is, so to speak, bereft of our original partner. Our *imperfection*, then, is our *incompleteness*, and seeking self-completion is the route (back) to perfection" (Rose, 1992, p. 67).

We consider this perspective in relation to Antonio Corelli's psychological growth as an artist who tries to attain self-completion through the re-union with the Mother archetype in his journey towards perfection symbolically represented by his artistic masterpiece.

Rose thinks that the artist is a person who goes back to the deeply rooted early experience of fusion during which he could "gain an increased apprehension of the nature of reality" (Rose, 1992, p. 69). This experience is not just a personal fantasy, but an examination of the primordial union states of maternal oneness and bisexuality, through which the artist has the privilege to "reshape reality in new forms" (Rose, 1992, p. 69). This re-appearance from an early state of fusion and the re-formation of the ego limits imply the prospect of perceiving a changed or an original arrangement of reality. The interaction with the Mother changes the manner in which the artist perceives reality.

In this respect, Gilbert J. Rose explains that

by making the work serve as a proxy, the artist can vicariously relive the primitive experiments of testing reality by repeated fusions and separations. The artwork is built up and melted down again and again, repeating second-hand the building up and melting down of psychic structure in the emergence from narcissism. In this way the artist can give him or herself up to the artwork, sometimes with the intensity of an addiction, and impress him or herself upon it in repeated alternations of active mastery and passive surrender, of controlled fusion, letting go and reimposing control, to rediscover depths and limits. The artist resamples the earliest body imagery, perhaps in an unconscious fantasy of fusion and rebirth. The intensity of instinctual forces is reduced as self - and object representations become further refined, more internalization takes place, and, in the process, additional psychic structure is built from further drive neutralization. In other words, the artist searches for self-completion in the work; he or she has a private dialogue with a projected part of self-mirroring, smiling, frowning, approaching, and withdrawing, until the final completion and release. (Rose, 1992, p. 73)

In light of Rose's words, we see our artist, Antonio Corelli, as being involved into a dialectical process with his artwork, giving new shapes to reality, as in the association "How like a woman is a mandolin" (De Bernières, 1995, p. 303). Since Rose depicts the interaction in which the artist creates his artwork as he creates himself, Corelli's dialogue with his art is important to us. It is interesting to examine how Corelli interacts with his artwork when narcissism appears as a *sine qua non* condition for creativity:

> I think of Pelagia in terms of chords. Antonia [the mandolin] has three cords that live together in the first three frets, *doh*, *re*, and *sol*, and they all need two fingers apiece to stop them. I play *sol*, and I move it one space across and I make the *doh*, and they ring in each other's aftermath like soprano and alto in the same key in a Tuscan song. I play the *re*, twisting my hand, making a double space, and it belongs with the other two, but it is sad and incomplete, it is like a virgin unfulfilled. It begs me 'Take me back where I can find my peace', and I return to *sol*, and all's complete, and I feel like God Himself who made a woman and found His world perfected by a final and a consummating touch. (De Bernières, 1995, p. 304)

The feeling of omnipotence has an essential role in the creative impulse. If in an early stage of the process of growth the experience of being all-powerful has given rise to some grandiose notions, later they become remodelled into perfectionist ambitions to which the artist aspires in his attempt to achieve self-respect.

As Gilbert J. Rose claims, "the artist endows his or her work with ego ideal of perfection" (Rose, 1992, p. 63).

But in order to attain self-respect and self-completion, in his itinerary to perfection the artist should emerge from the state of narcissism. The loss of perfection plays an important part in the process of individuation, as well as in the formation of self-experience. Antonio admits the following:

> we were happy together, sitting on this balcony shaded by bougainvillaea visited by bees, but now it is the war; the war has returned and Pelagia knits her brow and frowns. I want to say, 'I am sorry Pelagia, it was not my idea, it was not me who stole Ionia. (…) I am not a natural parasite.' But I can say no such thing, as Pelagia knows.

And she understands why I cannot say it, but still blames me for a lack of will. (De Bernières, 1995, p. 305)

The pleasure that the artist experiences in the process of creation is also essential for the formation of personality in the process of individuation. It contributes to the re-establishment of the ego boundaries which are crucial to the artist's attempt to give new forms to reality. The delight of the creative process has been frequently associated with a physical satisfaction.

In the case of an artist-musician, this relation becomes even more obvious, since the requirements of quality imply constant repetition, and the reward that the musician receives from playing goes far beyond the one which is obtained by the passive listeners. As R. A. Sharpe claims, "for the pianist, the physical exercise involved in playing the piano, the intimate connection with the instrument, the dance of the fingers across the keyboard, is very important" (Sharpe, 2004, p. 4).

The daily relation with the musical instrument becomes an obligatory part of the artist's life, "bodily gesture as well as sound", as Charles Rosen says, who also considers that the survival of piano music will be due to the physical pleasure that it confers to the player (Rosen, 2003).

A similar delight is to be depicted in the case of Antonio Corelli who experiences a strong bond with his musical instrument, called Antonia, and who extends the reality into a new form by comparing Antonia to his beloved woman:

'How like a woman is a mandolin, how gracious and how lovely. In the evening when the dogs howl and the crickets chirr (…) I take my sweet Antonia. I brush her strings, softly, and I say to her, 'How can you be made of wood?' just as I see Pelagia and ask without speaking, 'Are you truly made of flesh? Is there not here a fire? A vanishing trace of angels? A something far estranged from bone and blood?' (…) At night I dream of Pelagia. Pelagia comes, undressing, and I see her breasts are the backs of mandolins moulded in Napoli. I cup them in my hands and they are cold like wood and worm like yielding mother's flesh, and she turns about and I see that each buttock is the rounded pear-shaped singing mandolin, swelling in tapered segments, purfled in pearl and silvers of ebony. I am confused because I am caught between looking for strings and the pain of the loins' longing, and I wake up moistened by my own lust, clutching Antonia, pricked by the scratching ends of strings, sweating. I put Antonia down and say, 'O Pelagia,' and I lie awake awhile, thinking of her before I force myself asleep because then it will be morning sooner, and I will see Pelagia. (De Bernières, 1995, pp. 303–304)

Corelli's artwork is composed of the projected content of his psyche. The artist emerges into the act of self-creation through the means of both internal and external structure building. As Gilbert J. Rose explains, the creative activity resembles the act of the artist's growth and formation. Yet the act of artistic creation does not imply only the artist's own self. It also refers to the universal self-making process which is preserved in the artistic masterpiece. In this respect, Corelli explains his act of composition in the following:

> 'I am composing a march for you,' I say, 'listen,' and I play *re* minor, one two, and then *doh* major, one-and-two-and-, and back to *re* minor, one two ... and I tell her, 'The trouble is that I need another player to put a Greek melody over the top, perhaps a rebetiko of some sort. Maybe I can find someone in the battalion with a mandolin, and I can play the chords an octave lower on a mandola. I think that would sound very good.' (De Bernières, 1995, p. 305)

Although Corelli's artwork stems from his private fantasy, the form of his creative imagination transcends the personal and reforms the reality itself. As an Italian invader, Corelli drops completely this image of the self, restructuring the reality in a manner resembling the restructuring of the self. Composing a Greek melody dedicated to a Greek woman, he transcends the boundaries of his ego and consequently becomes capable of achieving an innovative arrangement of reality. Rose accurately claims that:

> A work of art simplifies but also expands and deepens the view of the world and of the self. As ego coordinated activity recapitulates the past in the light of the present to prepare for the future, the artwork summarizes and magnifies the process by which each of us continually tests and masters reality, relating inner and outer in repeated fusions and separations. The creative work that remains behind represents the cast of the mind "reborn" and objectified in the process of thought, feeling and action. (Rose, 1992, pp. 77–78)

While expanding his newly acquired view of the world and self, Corelli also extends this vision upon his battalion in an efficient manner, through music, making the others see reality from a completely different perspective. Corelli's ego re-evaluates the past from the perspective of the present in order to prepare for an uncertain future, whereas his masterpiece condenses and intensifies the process by which everyone tries to restructure the actual reality:

> I think again, 'How like a woman is a mandolin, how like Pelagia is a mandolin, how gracious and how lovely,' and I have the further thought, a paradox worthy of Xeno himself, that it was the war that brought us together and the war that prises us apart. The British call it 'giving with one hand and taking away with the other'. What have I got against the British that I have had to come to Greece? Pelagia is right, but who will be the first to say it? So far only Antonia has said it, ringing with 'Pelagia's March', singing beneath my fingers. (De Bernières, 1995, p. 307)

It is Pelagia's March that emerges as a newly "reborn" projection of the artist's mind, envisaging Corelli's thoughts, feelings, and actions. From this moment on, a new artwork exists, which has been created out of the fusion between the self-experience of Antonio and the world around him. After this artwork comes into existence, Corelli inspects and judges it, developing a dialogue between the created artwork, on one side, and the artist's subjectivity and judgment, on the other.

It is important to emphasize that a dualism occurs to represent two areas of self-experience: the internal (subjective) and the external (objective). In their interaction, both influence each other and this leads to a further creation. And if the artist is identified with his artwork, any further creation signifies further development and psychological growth of the artist.

Returning to the archetypal framework, Corelli's encounter with the goddess, incorporating the creative universal powers, proves to be beneficent to our quester-artist who, in search for beauty and artistic fulfilment, seems to have achieved his goal. The process of internal and psychological transformation enables the seeker-artist Corelli to continue his journey and prepares him for the next stage in his search for sublime.

The archetypal encounter with the Father, or so-called "atonement", represents an essential stage for individual development. In the case of Corelli, the Father figure encountered is not his biological father but Pelagia's father, Dr Iannis, who is a knowledgeable and wise man, definitely a parental and paternal figure able to initiate a person "into a larger world". Corelli's experience of "atonement" with the father is not to be understood in terms of a search for redemption.

In spite of the word's suggestion of the reparation for a sin, the word "atonement" is important to us by its meaning used in the Middle English language, which is that of "reconciliation" or being "at one". Consequently, Corelli's encounter with the father is, in fact, an encounter with his own self. The similarity between the father and Corelli is clearly stated in the novel through Corelli's words revealing his understanding of it:

> you and I are very alike. I am obsessed by music, and you are obsessed with your medicine. We are both men who have created a purpose for ourselves, and neither of us cares very much for what anyone else may think of us. [Pelagia] has only been able to love me because she learned first how to love another man who is like me. And that man is you. So being a Greek or an Italian is incidental. (De Bernières, 1995, p. 355)

Far from being competitive, the relationship between Dr Iannis and Corelli is rather fulfilling. Their cooperation is obvious in the episode in which Antonio removes the broken strings from his mandolin and laments upon the impossibility of finding new ones, while Dr Iannis suggests the replacing of those strings with surgical wires. This moment symbolically refers to Dr Iannis' acceptance of Corelli as his son, or rather, a part of his own self. The surgical wires entwine the two of them forever, by which the much desired harmony is attained, and this harmony contributes to an integrated sense of identity for both characters.

But in order to attain a complete sense of identity, Corelli has to acknowledge that he is truly in a transpersonal and transcultural context. Relying on the symbolical suggestion that the doctor and Corelli represent reflections of each other's ego, Dr Iannis initiates Corelli into understanding the sense of being a Greek:

> Don't you remember asking me why it is that Greeks smile when they are angry? Well, let me tell you something, young man. Every Greek, man, woman, and child, has two Greeks inside. We even have technical terms for them. They are part of us, as inevitable as the fact that we all write poetry and the fact that every one of us thinks that he knows everything that there is to know. (De Bernières, 1995, p. 357)

In fact, Dr Iannis tries to explain to Antonio that there is darkness inside all people, an unknown side that is hidden and unpredictable. Corelli must acknowledge the existence of this secret side as a part of his own self and defeat it in order to be able to continue his artistic enterprise. As a result, Antonio tries to surpass his personal desires, traversing the transpersonal and the transcultural reality to find the harmony with his own self. But this inner harmony can be attained only by truly understanding one's mission in life.

In the process of acknowledgment of one's mission in life, the paternal figure is of essential importance. In the case of an artist, from psychoanalytical point of view, the paternal imago could be considered as the source of the sublime. Beauty, as an aesthetic experience, has been frequently associated with maternal image. As George Hagman explains,

> the normal tendency to experience the mother as special becomes elaborated and structuralized as idealization: the mother is idealized, the self-in-relation to the mother is idealized, and the relationship is idealized. In addition, the formal aspects of such idealization (the mother's touch; the sound of her voice; the rhythm of her words [...]) become highly valued sensations that coalesce and crystallize into an aesthetic sensibility, which is gradually articulated and elaborated into mature forms of aesthetic experience, such as the sense of beauty. (Hagman, 2005, p. 131)

In the process of development, the father becomes a part of the aesthetic space that the mother has established and cultivated for the child. Of course, the father also evolves into an object which is idealized by the youngster. This process presupposes the interchange and extension of value effects that endow the representation of the father, self, and the relationship of a high regard and admiration. While together, the father and his child experience mutually an increased contentment, an elevated self-esteem, energy, and joy. Concurrently, this relation may reveal a strong excitement, fear, admiration and sublimity. Hagman again:

> Paternal idealizations that crystallize out of these affective exchanges acquire a different tone from the maternal idealization, and this will, to a large extent, determine the unique combination of affective responses that compose the paternal aesthetic experience. The father is experienced as loved but feared, intimate but expansive, familiar but complex, accessible but immense – in other words, an entire range of often-contradictory experiences that lend a remarkable intensity to paternal aesthetic sensibility. (Hagman, 2005, p. 133)

Symbolically, the sense of beauty, represented in the novel by Pelagia, provides an aesthetic experience where reality is perceived, by Corelli, as both ideal and harmonious with his inner life. In his process of development, Antonio moves out of an enclosed, balanced and clearly aesthetic space of the mother into an open, powerful, unrestrained but dynamic commitment with the world as introduced by the doctor-father. Dr Iannis tells Corelli: "You would have to live here, that's all. If she went to Italy she would die of homesickness. I know my daughter. You might have to choose between loving her and becoming a musician" (De Bernières, 1995, p. 358).

In a way, Dr Iannis stimulates Corelli's fantasies provided by the father's power and omnipotence. He is the one to open new horizons for Antonio beyond and outside the dyadic relation which is experienced with Pelagia. His awareness of a reality outside the one created with Pelagia intrinsically combines in an aesthetics of admiration and sublimity.

Dr Iannis, as a paternal imago, has the role of stimulating the psychological separation process, in which Corelli's inner and outer worlds grow to be individuated. The doctor attempts to create some favourable circumstances for Antonio's self-development, contributing, therefore, to Antonio's acknowledgement of new forms of interpersonal experiences. As Hagman claims, "in regard to aesthetics, (…) the father offers distinctly different ways of structuring and giving form to interactions. This alternative aesthetic creates experiences of newness and stimulates the child's excitement and creativity" (Hagman, 2005, p. 133).

In other words, the contradictory feelings produced by the paternal aesthetic represent the foundational part of the sublime experience, because it encourages the artist to seek out the innovation and uniqueness, and, at the same time, it provides an opportunity to explore the world.

This unique opportunity opens when Corelli descends to the underworld. Symbolically, the descent motif is presented in the massacre episode. It is now that Antonio Corelli, surviving miraculously the massacre and having had the broken ribs mended with four strings from the mandolin by Dr Iannis, reveals a sense of vitality and potency without precedent. In archetypal terms, the atonement with the father refers to the stage of re-joining the great circle of life, which signifies the discovery of one's place in the universe. The strings of the mandolin, in the case of Corelli, unify symbolically the unconscious and the consciousness, a union which represents the accomplishment of his wholeness. Corelli acknowledges his existence as a quintessence of the transpersonal world, his true Self, in the realm of the sublime, produced by his music, and understands that this is his true heroic mission, his place in the universe.

Orpheus produces his best artistic expression only after having completed the experience of the descent into the underworld. Similarly, Corelli discovers now a universe of fresh experiences, and he feels simultaneously fear, wonder, and astonishment, and, out of these contradictory feelings, new forms, new styles, the ever-expanding sounds, and perpetual innovation are achieved. This newly discovered capacity to create takes him outward into a reality which is at once awesome and exhilarating. As he explains later in the novel,

> I realized that I was completely old-fashioned, so that I had to find another way to be innovative. Do you know what I did? I took old folk tunes, like some Greek ones, and I set them for unusual instruments. My second concerto has Irish pipes and a banjo in it, and guess what? The critics loved it. Actually it's in exactly the same form, with the same kind of development, as you would find in Mozart or Haydn or whatever. It sounds good too. I'm just a trickster waiting to be found out. I specialize in finding new ways to be an anachronism. (De Bernières, 1995, p. 525)

The descent into the realm of death provides the opportunity to confront his dark and hidden aspects of the Self and to ascend to the superior realm of the sublime. This sublime experienced by Corelli proves to be stimulating and self-confirming. It is somehow the coarseness of the effect, infused by separation, sense of loss, combined with the passion of fantasy centred on Pelagia, and the shock produced by the new, which is contained and exposed within a formal structure of his music, and which is experienced as extraordinary, amazing, and ultimately transcendental.

The sense of the sublime represents Corelli's ultimate blessing, his elixir of life. As he claims, "it's the enthusiasm [produced by the sublime] that keeps me alive" (De Bernières, 1995, p. 525). Therefore, the "refusal of return", in Jungian terms, seems to be natural in the case of our quester-artist. His dilemma about homecoming reveals his supreme delight experienced by the attainment of the sublime. This state of the sublime is described by Hagman in the following terms:

> Even while a sense of security is maintained, the normal confines of the self are fantastically expanded and psychological boundaries disappear. We are temporarily and

nontraumatically overwhelmed, and there is a feeling of selflessness accompanied by a pleasurable anxiety. Unlike the oceanic feeling, this is not comforting, but disruptive; the self is carried away in the rough water – over the falls, so to speak – captured by the current. This amalgamation of anxiety and pleasure is a special feature of the sublime. (Hagman, 2005, p. 141)

Due to this supreme state attained by Corelli during his journey of self-discovery, he refuses to return, since the return would signify to him the re-joining of the ordinary, waking consciousness. Instead, he prefers to remain immersed in the elevated state of consciousness, produced by the experience of the sublime. His reluctance to leave this state can be explained again in Hagman's terms:

the sublime functions to bring a number of different terrors within a containable, ordered universe. It is the powerful discharge of desire and aggression without catastrophe; it can portray the results of discharge without the destruction of the self or loved one. Death, sexuality, aggression, loss of self, vulnerability, and isolation are embraced and overcome (yet not by being negated or denied). Paradoxically, the experience of these terrors in the sublime is vitalizing and self-comforting, not disorganizing. There is an emotional state of arousal/tranquillity. (Hagman, 2005, p. 142)

It is now that Corelli explores the entire world with an intensified sense of curiosity, examining new challenges and engaging into new aesthetic experiences that would result in new forms, new artworks. The reviews by important critics and experts of Corelli's work are presented in the novel:

This, the long awaited reissue of Antonio Corelli's first concerto for mandolin and small orchestra, was first published in 1954, and premiered in Milan, with the composer playing the soloist's part. It was inspired by, and dedicated to, a woman named in the score only as 'Pelagia'. The main theme, scored in 2/2 time, is stated very clearly and emphatically on the solo instrument after a brief flourish on woodwind. It is a simple and martial melody that was described by one of its earliest reviewers as "artfully naïve". In the first movement it is developed in sonata form (…) (De Bernières, 1995, p. 527)

By creating a self-actualized identity, Corelli becomes, in a way, the "master of two worlds", which allows him to experience complete control over his own destiny. By having harmonized the powerful forces of the unconscious that generally devastate the rational self or the ego, Corelli, after his return, assumes the role of a leader who must transform his world. After an absence of about fifty years, Corelli comes back to Cephallonia, reunites with Pelagia, plans to reconstruct the old house, and, what is mostly important, he will teach young Iannis to play the mandolin and the meaning of music.

In terms of the monomythic experience, Corelli performs a journey, seeking a double boon, which is both personal and public. Starting with his earliest experiences in life, he has perceived knowledge about himself as well as about the world in which he has lived as expressed in music. But once having achieved the supreme knowledge, he creates his own music, which expresses his own idea of the universe: a harmonious and balanced environment, in which the only power and control applied are upon a musical instrument and an aesthetic experience. In this way, Corelli becomes useful to his community by exposing to new generations his values which are revealed in his music and which have gained world acclaim.

In this respect, we consider that the monomyth of the hero and the quest exceeds the simple frame of self-individuation. The quester and his achievements should be viewed as part of a larger frame – the community and the universe – a whole that delineates and forms the hero almost as the hero is the image of that community or universe. Consequently, Corelli's attained sense of supreme joy and of the sublime which harmonizes his inner world can affect the sense of joyfulness and equilibrium which is experienced by people around him.

However, Corelli as a hero is completely reimagined. Louis de Bernières creates a unique individual from a totally unheroic perspective, and he seems to redefine the concept of heroism from an opposite viewpoint. His unheroic hero Corelli is an artist with a mostly attractive personality and a completely new vision of the world. De Bernières' hero, Antonio Corelli, consumes all his martial ambitions through his music and composes marches with variations on the same theme. The novelist suggests that the heroic image and ideal should be revised and become more inclusive, where the hero could be an artist-musician who should be admired for his virtuosity in playing a musical instrument, and who by his music crosses all cultural and language barriers, attaining a state of a "citizen of this world", of peace and harmony all over the world.

Louis de Bernières subverts certain traditional monomythic conventions, as well as the image of the hero, but he still preserves their general framework with the purpose to make the reader oppose the convention with the revised type and develop a new awareness of the world. Thus, while rethinking the monomythic experience, de Bernières presents a hero who is not interested in bloodshed or the conquering of a territory; his understanding of domination is expressed only in terms of music, only as an artist dominating the world by his artwork.

Another convention of the monomyth refers to the return of the hero to the homeland after the completion of his mission. The novelist subverts this convention as well, because his hero, Corelli, returns to a place which does not represent his initial position. He returns to a land which was invaded by his army, where he was once one of the oppressors, but who expands it into a homeland due to his great love, his capacity of going beyond any cultural borders, and also due to the fact that this land has propelled him to the awareness of his own self, an awareness that provides him with a sense of the sublime and reifies his accomplishment as both an individual and an artist.

Also, if the traditional hero completes his circle with his journey, Corelli's trajectory is spiral or cyclic, or ever-open-ended, which is suggesting a perpetual return. This aspect could be considered as having an optimistic implication, since each of Corelli's arrivals to Cephallonia ends in love, communion, and, eventually, in the creation of new music that would be listened to by his community with a supreme delight, and the people would be succumbing to the pleasure of this music, forgetting, hopefully, all the negative aspects of existence.

The final convention of the monomyth, however, namely that the journey is revealed as a paradigm for individual's psychic and spiritual growth, is respected in the case of Antonio Corelli. Louis de Bernières exposes a protagonist who behaves always in accordance with his consciousness. Throughout his long life and implicit journeys Corelli is represented as a good-natured young man, trying to spread love and joy in his living environment, although there has been a war. He succeeds in overpowering his instincts or the negative aspects of his own self in situations which are most complicated and dangerous, cultivating his personality through humanity, dignity, honour, and love.

This is his *arête*, his excellence and for this he is to be admired. His psychic and spiritual growth represents a complete success, because he never fails to live according to his well-established system of values. In a way, Louis de Bernières seems to suggest that the victory of the human being can be achieved only when the individual does not deviate from the system of values and morality, because these elements represent the only organizing principle in otherwise chaotic and random postmodern universe.

2.3.3 Pelagia

We have already revealed that Louis de Bernières' *Captain Corelli's Mandolin* has as its central metaphor the traditional journey of the hero, and, despite deconstructing or subverting its frame, the journey is still present at the heart of the novel. Of course, the novelist has inverted the traditional hero model with an anti-heroic one, since an extensive scepticism has resulted from the failures of most of the traditional heroic enterprises.

This situation creates a paradox, because one would think about the necessity of depicting the heroic after revealing an anti-heroic mood. In this respect, Sidney Hook claims the following:

It may mean that we still believe in heroes and their important role in history, but lament their absence in our time and our place. This is presupposed when we ask "where have all the heroes gone?" and is implied in the answer some offer that "they have been slain by our mediocrity." It indicates a belief not only in the possibility of heroic action but in its desirability. (Hook, 1978, p. 4)

In his attempt to deconstruct the conventional heroic mood, Louis de Bernières demythologizes the image of the hero, creating instead different and original alternatives to the heroic. He uses the term "hero" mostly in order to refer to a man or a woman of unique achievements, or to depict an ordinary person who is admired and greatly respected in a community during some crucial moments of this societal existence.

These new types of heroes, as presented by Louis de Bernières, become highly appreciated "for the risks taken beyond the call of duty, their quiet sacrifice, their fortitude in adversity, their refusal to compromise with corruption, or their independence of vision or judgement" (Hook, 1978, p. 6).

The novelist tries to redefine the hero also in terms of gender, inviting the reader to a reflection upon the heroic which is performed in a domestic environment, contrary to the conventional heroism on the battlefield.

From the moment of publication of Joseph Campbell's heroic quest paradigm, presented in *The Hero with a Thousand Faces*, there have been created many alternatives to it, especially concerning female heroines. Although Campbell asserts that the monomyth is the same for heroes as well as for heroines, on a closer inspection, however, not many similarities could be discovered, since, as Nadya Aisenberg explains, the heroine's journey does not consist of "replacing heroes with heroines within a male epic or tragedy, with acts of physical bravery as milestones, taking place in time which is successional" (Aisenberg, 1994, p. 38). In fact, it reveals a completely different pattern.

It is worth mentioning here the contribution of the psychotherapist and mythologist Maureen Murdock who, among others, has tried and succeeded to reconfigure Campbell's heroic pattern for women. From her practice of psychology, Murdock has noticed that many women embarking on the traditional heroic quest model end up in frustration, which is provoked by their willingness to become "pseudo-male". This situation emerges in an environment which is based on patriarchal ideology, and which confers higher value to men's achievements and masculine qualities, depreciating or ignoring the achievements and qualities of women.

As a result of this condition, women "start to define themselves in terms of deficits, in terms of what they don't have or haven't accomplished, and begin to obscure and devalue themselves as women" (Murdock, 1990, p. 14). Murdock considers that the true heroic quest, in the case of women, is to turn inward and "fully embrace their feminine nature", and seek for a more affirming life paradigm that will integrate and evaluate both masculine and feminine aspects of their personalities, and thus become balanced, whole human beings (Murdock, 1990, p. 3).

Consequently, Louis de Bernières creates a new face or hypostasis of the hero, which is actually a heroine as a young woman from a village in Cephallonia, thus reimagining and rewriting the monomyth of the hero and the quest from gender perspectives as well. Working within a male traditional frame of the monomyth, de Bernières transcends gender borders by presenting an unusual young woman, Pelagia, who lives in an ordinary environment. She is unusual in that she is brought up only by her father, Dr Iannis, who has raised her in a quite unorthodox manner.

In this environment, all young women are educated according to the traditional definitions of femininity, namely those of becoming good wives and good mothers for the household. Pelagia, apart from the customary obligations of the house, is taught by her father to read and write, is fluent in both Italian and Katharevousa, enjoys the reading of poetry, is educated to reflect upon everything in her world and to take her own decisions, and, what is mostly atypical, possesses sufficient knowledge in medicine. Such an unexpected female type depicted in a conventional patriarchal environment becomes baffling, especially in the context of the monomyth of the hero and the quest, which is seen as a process of growth and development. How should such an unusual woman develop under these circumstances is the natural question upon which the reader is invited to reflect.

Certainly, Louis de Bernières feminizes the monomyth, although Jung presents only masculine inclusion into the process of individuation. We see that the novelist challenges also the conventional tripartite structure – departure-adventure-return – depicting his heroine as a local inhabitant from Cephallonia who never moves away from her island, her journey being envisaged completely in psychological terms.

From her first appearance in the novel, Pelagia does not acknowledge her need for self-development or self-assertion. Apparently, she seems to be concerned only with the typical aspects of life of all other young women of her age: find her love and become a wife and a mother. This situation is not surprising, since, according to Carol Pearson, "women are more likely initially to seek identity in relationship and to place great value on caring for others" (Pearson, 1991, p. 260). These aspects become a great challenge in Pelagia's life, and her relation to Mandras seems to be promising to help her develop her boundaries and satisfy her need of taking care of others. She exposes an ardent desire to see her lover:

> Where is Mandras? He is usually here by now. I want him to come. I can hardly breathe, I want him to come so much. My hands are shaking again. I'd better take this silly smile off my face, or everyone will think that I'm mad. Come, Mandras, please come (...). Stay for dinner, and stroke my shin with your feet, Mandras. (De Bernières, 1995, p. 83)

Her intention is to create a kind of "web", as Pearson says, aiming at the collective welfare or "the good of everyone within that web" (Pearson, 1991, p. 261). Pelagia imagines that a happy family life with her loving husband may provide her with supreme satisfaction. Such a premise emerges as logical to her, since this is the model of existence to which all the young ladies in her community aspire.

Also, Pelagia lives in a family in which the mother figure is absent, and throughout her entire existence, she has witnessed her father's yearning for his lost wife. Observing daily her father's craving for her dead mother, Pelagia assumes that building a family web of affection and care would make her experience supreme delight, and she understands her identity only in relation to family life.

Pelagia acknowledges clearly the necessity of establishing a strong family net, and, at the same time, she is brought up by her father to be inquisitive about everything happening around her.

As a consequence of these two diverging perspectives, although she identifies herself with the family web, she is also extremely curious about her own identity and her place and role in universe and community.

Pelagia's first investigation about her identity concerns sexuality. The burning desire that she experiences is a completely new sensation:

> I like [Mandras'] backside, God forgive me, even though I've never seen it. I can just tell that I like it. That I would like it. It's very small. When he bends down I can see that it's like two halves of a melon. I mean, the curves seem to be in a proportion according to God's original design for fruit. When he kisses me I want to reach round him and take a buttock in each hand. I never have. I wouldn't. What would he say if I did? I have such sluttish thoughts. Thank God no one reads my mind, I would be locked up and all the old women would throw stones at me and call me a whore. When I think of Mandras I get a picture of his face, grinning, and then I get a picture of him bending over. (De Bernières, 1995, p. 77)

She understands that this sexual desire makes her feel different; it confuses and startles her because she cannot hold control over the situation.

Pelagia's sexual awakening represents at once her symbolical separation from her previous image of the self and the embarking on a journey towards the exploration of her true self. As Coline Covington states, "both [boys and girls] share a basic need to separate and must achieve this by exploring how they differ and how they are similar – through opposition and identification" (Covington, 1989, p. 252).

At this stage of her development, Pelagia understands naively that the way in which she differs from a man is only from the anatomical perspective, and this is where she begins her exploration:

> Sometimes I wonder if I'm normal, but the things the women say when we are all together and the men are in the kapheneion. If the men only knew, what a shock! Every woman in the village knows that Kokolios' penis is curved sideways like a banana and that the priest has a rash on his scrotum, and the men don't know. They don't have a clue what we talk about (...). And when we find a potato that looks like a set of men's equipment we pass it round and laugh about it. (De Bernières, 1995, p. 77)

Although Pelagia acts intuitively, like most women of her community who examine their differences from men in terms of anatomy, she conceives of another difference in that, while thinking of gender distinctions, she does not limit them to anatomy but examines the social roles of men and women in community.

Contrary to most women that live in humility and submission, Pelagia is inquisitive and exhibits enough faith in her own self. While reflecting upon the necessity of bringing water to the house, she reveals her displeasure at carrying it all by herself, asking "where is it written down that women have to carry water when they are stronger? When Mandras asks me to marry him, I am going to say, 'Not unless you agree to fetch the water'" (De Bernières, 1995, p. 78). At the same time, she is preoccupied with the contribution that one should bring to the world, saying: "What we need is an inventor to come and put in a pump to take the water to the house" (De Bernières, 1995, p. 78).

We understand that Pelagia's concern is not limited to the investigation of her own identity; her preoccupation is of social nature as well. Within a social world of men, a dominating traditional patriarchal society, most women are in a state of dependency developing only the capacity of forming inner connections, and thus acting passively, but Pelagia tries to change her status of dependency by her quest for an identity which is both sexual and social. Although her desire for personal autonomy and self-assertion is limited and refers only to her domination by her father or lover, she never feels under-evaluated by either of them. She reveals enough strength to rebel against any overly masculine behaviour of Mandras or against the dominant attitude of her father when she claims:

> I could kill Papas. What does he mean, telling Mandras that I won't have a dowry? Who marries without one? Papas says that it's a barbarism, and they don't do it in any civilized country he knows of, and you should marry for love as he did, and that it's an obscenity to make it a transaction, and that it implies that a woman is not worth marrying unless she carries property on her back. Well, then I'll be forced to marry a foreigner if he thinks like that. (De Bernières 1995, p. 78)

This fragment exhibits Pelagia's unbalanced self, as she struggles consciously against any form of dominance, but unconsciously undervalues herself by revealing her acceptance of objectification in the social world of men, in which a wife would be evaluated in terms of a dowry. She experiences a sense of inner disturbance, because she reacts unconsciously as any other woman, and identifies herself with her mother image that "has [an] internalized sense of inferiority or limitation", and, unconsciously, imitates the paradigm of the mother who is "trivialized by others" (Pearson, 1991, p. 258).

But having her mother dead, and, consequently, the mother model absent or reduced considerably, as well as being brought up by her father who has always encouraged her to accept her own worth and exert her own freedom of will, Pelagia acknowledges and reacts immediately to any form of oppression or dependency. This fact reveals that Pelagia has not attained an inner balance yet, and its absence represents one of the sources of her inadequacy.

Although operating within the net of her dependency upon men, Pelagia develops a sense of separate identity which is cautiously encouraged by her father throughout her entire life. For instance, while thinking of her relation with Mandras in terms of a major priority in her existence, she is not completely overwhelmed by her passion and consciously examines her fiancé's intellectual capacities:

> He is not a serious fellow, and it gives me doubts. He's so funny, but I can't talk to him about anything. You have to be able to discuss things with a husband, don't you? Everything is a joke with him. He is witty, and that shows that he's not stupid, I hope. I say, 'Is there going to be a war?' and he just grins and says, 'Who cares? Is there going to be a kiss?' I don't want there to be a war. Let there not be a war. (De Bernières, 1995, p. 82)

Pelagia constantly tries to build her identity upon the archetypal caregiver in terms of "connection"; intuitively, however, she develops her seeker identity when she reveals her constant curiosity about the world in which she lives:

> I could just sit here for hours watching the clouds unfolding about the summit of the mountain. I wonder where they come from? I mean, I know that it's just water vapour, but they just seem to gather together out of nothing quite suddenly. It's as if every drop has a secret to share with its brothers, and so they rise up out of the sea and huddle together and drift along in the breeze, and the clouds change shapes as the drops hurry from on confidante to another, whispering. They are saying, 'I can see Pelagia down there, sitting on the privy, and she doesn't even know that we are talking about her.' They are saying, 'I saw Pelagia and Mandras kissing. What will come of it? She would blush if she knew.' O, I am blushing. I am stupid. And why do the clouds travel more slowly than the wind that drives them? And why, sometimes,

does the wind blow one way and the clouds travel in another? Is Papakis right when he says that there are several layers of wind, or is it that the clouds have some means of traveling against it? I must cut up some more clouts, I have those pains in my stomach and my back, and it's about time. I saw the new moon last night, and that means I'm due. (De Bernières, 1995, p. 75)

Pelagia seems to be enwrapped into the web of family relations, obsessed with being in love, making connections and valuing greatly compassion and the caring for others. The model of nurturance, although acceptable at first for Pelagia, does not satisfy her hunger for exploring the world, understanding what rules govern this world, and primarily, perceiving what is her place and role in this world. Even while dreaming of Mandras, her horizon is expanded immediately, revealing her yearning to know herself as well as her universe.

Although Pelagia is trying to conceal her quester or seeker side in a patriarchal environment, this aspect of her personality is noticed by people in her community. It is Mandras, her fiancé, first, who recognizes openly her superiority: "'Siora, will you marry me? Marry me or I die.' 'Why do you call me Siora?' she asked. 'Because you speak Italian and sometimes wear a hat'" (De Bernières, 1995, p. 95). These words do not stem from a conventional behaviour of a lover willing to impress the lady of his heart. Mandras is aware of Pelagia's innate superiority, and, although he does not know how to explain it, he admits it and it becomes one of the most frustrating aspects of his existence. Pelagia, on the other hand, never attempts to express or prove her pre-eminence, and feels inadequate again, because her superiority shatters her understanding of dependence which is still essential for her existence.

Due to her individual nature of a caregiver, Pelagia truly wants to integrate into a whole, a web of family life that would make her feel complete. She is extremely captivated by her understanding of accomplishment in terms of family fulfilment, and fails to see beyond her fantasy which is built around Mandras:

> every train of memory twisted on its track and returned to that handsome boy on his knees by the bench where she sat, Mandras on his knees in a pool of wine, Mandras, so beautiful, luminous, and young; Mandras as exquisite as Apollo. Perspiration broke out on her limbs as she imagined herself entwined in his embrace, transformed him into an incubus, moved her arms and legs, caressed his back and experienced in absentia the soft curl of his tongue on her breasts and the lithe pressure of his weight. (De Bernières, 1995, p. 99)

Her excessive willingness to become a part of an amorous relationship makes her fall in love with her fantasy instead of the man. The object of her desire becomes projected from her imagination and it holds a considerable control over her.

Pelagia's imprisonment by her desire can be considered in terms of descent into the underworld which prevents her from the quest for self-accomplishment and the attaining of the Self. Nevertheless, although conforming to the norms of patriarchal community with regards to marriage and family relations, Pelagia is not completely dominated by them. She fights with the inner infernal dragons in order to free herself from the captivity in the underworld. Acting according to her inquisitive nature, she starts questioning these norms, as well as her fantasy:

> Marriage was such a big thing, it meant giving up one life for another. It meant leaving her father's house, it meant childbirth and relentless work in place of this gentle idyll with its mock contretemps, its tranquil routines, and its congenial eccentricities. She bridled at the thought of accepting orders and decisions from anyone but her own father, whose commands, however brusque and peremptory, were really requests ironically disguised. What would Mandras be like? How much did she really know him? What evidence did she have that he was patient and humane? He brought gifts, that was sure, but would the gifts not stop when the bargain was secured? Wasn't he too young and too full of impulses? There was something too decisive about his movements, his unconsidered responses; can you trust someone who replies immediately, without thought? Someone whose actions and words are poetic rather that solidly cogitated? (De Bernières, 1995, p. 99)

These hesitations, provoked by her seeker side, lead to a further unbalance which makes her feel disintegrated and out of place. These new experiences of being in love, of ardent desire felt by her body, and of proposed marriage become extremely tempting for Pelagia, since she has got accustomed to satisfy her curiosity in various new areas. But in parallel to this rising curiosity about a new phase in her existence, she feels overwhelmed, possessed, and as losing control over herself.

As a consequence, together with extreme excitement, Pelagia feels unhappiness and discontent with the present situation: "She thought of the capricious joie de vivre of the pine marten, its innocence and its complete absorption in the business of being itself, and realized quite suddenly that she had exchanged the carelessness of youth for something very like unhappiness" (De Bernières, 1995, p. 100).

Pelagia acknowledges that marriage signifies a separation from her usual environment and customary behaviours, and feels a kind of nostalgia for the happy childhood, the lost golden time of her innocence, and the lost tranquillity of her home in the secure company of her father. At the same time, she experiences fear at the thought that this separation would imply a partition from her inner self, because she will be obliged to conform to the authority of others instead of being herself. This sense of separation produce such a profound change that she finds herself imagining "that Mandras has died, and as the tears came she was shocked to discover that she also felt relief" (De Bernières, 1995, p. 100).

Pelagia becomes aware that the marriage she has desired so much and the family web that she has aspired to, do not correspond to her inner urge of searching for a separate identity. The conformity to the patriarchal norms of her community prevents her from experiencing the exploration of her own potential and the sense of self. She gradually starts to acknowledge that what she truly wants from life does not correspond to the ideal of womanhood.

Symbolically, Pelagia experiences an entire war which consumes her both spiritually and psychologically, a war between what she yearns for and her conformity to conventional existence. Pelagia's war can be described in heroic terms, since she is aware of the difference between her and the others in her environment; although she acknowledges her difference, she struggles much to fit into the kind of life assigned to her by the conventions.

Curiously, Pelagia's inner struggle parallels the one in the actual war, since her private war corresponds to the period of Mandras' participation in the war of independence. The novelist emphasises the link between the real battlefield and the fight that one performs during his or her lifetime. Pelagia is not depicted as many archetypal women are, women that assume the role of wives waiting passively for their heroes who are supposed to return victoriously from the battle. While Mandras is fighting for his country, Pelagia experiences her personal, inner war, a war of self-determination.

Louis de Bernières does not devalue this kind of war. On the contrary, to him the war of personal independence seems to have greater value, because by struggling against conformism and dependence on tradition, one can achieve a true sense of the self. Being true to oneself confers more honour and dignity to the individual than any other luring ideals.

Pelagia's first struggle for independence is revealed when she reacts against her dependency upon her father by taking the decision to make her own dowry. In a letter to Mandras, she declares: "I hope that you will be glad to know that I have decided to make my own dowry. I think that my father has no sense of shame, and sometimes I feel very angry with him for refusing the very thing that is normal for every other girl" (De Bernières, 1995, pp. 128–129).

This moment clearly delineates a split between her dependency upon her father and her unconscious search for independence. Of course, in her naivety, she is not aware that she simply replaces one dependency by another one, a convention by another convention. However, it is important to emphasize this aspect of separation as a clearly acknowledged fact, as a moment that marks her determination to search for identity.

Maureen Murdock, who has elaborated on the model of the heroine's journey in search of identity, refers to this moment as "Separation from the Feminine"

(Murdock, 1990). She considers that this separation generally reveals a rejection of some traditionally feminine aspects of existence, such as passivity, dependence, powerlessness, weakness, acceptance of manipulation, and lack of purpose. Pelagia's journey in search of her identity begins with a rejection of obedience and limitations, but while rebelling against these traditional feminine aspects of existence, she does not distantiate herself from the Feminine. On the contrary, in her rebelliousness, she engages in some feminine acts unknown to her prior to this crucial moment in her life. In her letters, she explains to Mandras:

> I began to crochet a big cover for our marriage bed, but I had to unpick it because it went wrong and began to look like a dead animal. I am no good at womanly things because my mother died when I was too young, and now I am having to try to learn all the things that I should have grown up with. I am beginning with things for the bed, because that is where our life will begin, but afterwards, I will make other things for the house to use on feast days and for when we have visitors. I get very bored with the crochet, but my comfort is that when you return you will find all the evidence of my love before you. I am thinking that it would be a fine thing if I made you a waistcoat embroidered with gold thread and flowers made in festoon and fil-tirè so that you flash in the sunlight when you dance. (De Bernières, 1995, p. 129)

In her search for identity, Pelagia is looking for a proper feminine role model to be imitated by her throughout her spiritual journey. Her mother would be a proper guide, but facing her absence, Pelagia wonders astray alone, her loneliness increasing her sense of inadequacy. However, since "many mothers offer their daughters passive, diminished models of femaleness", even nowadays (Pipher, 1994, p. 252), be Pelagia's mother alive and present, by her submissive and lacking initiative status, the mother would indicate clearly to her daughter that she should behave similarly.

Clarissa Pinkola Estés goes further, claiming that in the stories about heroines in which a "too-good" mother exists, this mother should die before she would affect the girl's development: "The ever-watching, hovering, protective psychic mother is not adequate as a central guide for one's future instinctual life (…) taking on the task of being on one's own, developing one's consciousness (…). As the too-good mother dies, the new woman is born" (Estés, 1992, p. 81).

Similarly, in the absence of her mother, Pelagia emerges as a new woman, relying on herself in her search for independence and personal accomplishment. Also, on her way to personal fulfilment, she relies on the role model provided by her father. The paternal figure has been always considered to be of essential importance in the process of growth of a child. In the case of the development of a young girl, this figure becomes even more crucial, since it assumes the responsibility of representing the opposite sex. Linda Leonard explains: "He is the first masculine figure in her life and is a prime shaper of the way she relates to the masculine side of herself and ultimately to men. Since he is "other", i.e., different from herself and her mother, he also shapes her differentness, her uniqueness and individuality" (Leonard, 1982, p. 11).

Due to the impact of her father, Pelagia has grown to respect herself, be inquisitive, explore the universe, as well as strive to know herself. Her father is the first who depicts his daughter's uniqueness; he is the first to educate her to acknowledge her own worth. As Leonard claims, "the father also projects ideals for his daughter. He provides a model for authority, responsibility, decision-making, objectivity, order, and discipline" (Leonard, 1982, p. 11). Pelagia assimilates all these principles from her father, valuing and applying them throughout her journey of self-fulfilment.

Maureen Murdock names this phase in the development of the heroine as "Identification with the Masculine and Gathering of Allies". Since most girls try to find an identity through identification and connection, in the absence of a mother, it is most likely to connect and identify with the father. As Murdock claims, in the process of maturation, there are certain positive aspects of a daughter's identification with the masculine characteristics of her father:

> Seeking male validation is a healthy transition from fusion with the mother to great independence in a patriarchal society. The young woman who identifies with what could be considered positive father qualities, such as discipline, decision-making, direction, courage, power, and self-valuation, finds herself achieving success in the world. (Murdock, 1990, p. 37)

As a consequence, in her rebelliousness against her dependence on her father by asserting her feminine aspects, such as being a nurturing, loving person and doing the most feminine acts of crocheting and embroidery, Pelagia soon discovers that she is easily bored by these activities and fails to complete them. Pelagia explains in her letters to Mandras: "I have started the waistcoat for you, but I have had to unpick the bedcover again because it was coming out even worse than before. I don't know what's wrong with me" (De Bernières, 1995, p. 131).

This also symbolizes her struggle to remain in the realm of the Feminine concomitantly with the desire to act like a man.

Actually, during this period of waiting for Mandras to return from the war, Pelagia carries her own fight, which is that of struggling and sustaining her woman's femininity, her sense of self as a woman against her sense of a seeker and accomplisher. She soon acknowledges this inner struggle and reveals it by the following statement:

I got halfway through the bedcover, but then Psipsina was sick on it, and I had to wash it. It didn't shrink, thanks be to God, but when I laid it out to dry the goat ate three mouthfuls from the middle. I was so angry that I actually beat it with a broomstick, and the Papas came out and found me in a storm of tears. I hit him too. You should have seen the look on his face. Anyway, I unpicked it yet again, and saved as much wool as I could, but I'm beginning to think that fate wants me to make something else. (De Bernières, 1995, p. 133)

Pelagia's explosion of rage represents the despair that she experiences when realizing that she is unfit for such domestic activities, unfit for the family life that she has projected in her fantasies. The blame she lays upon fate represents her fear of admitting that she is not adequate for this kind of life and for her relation with Mandras, and she is yearning for the possibility of exploring the world instead. This aspect becomes obvious when one of her passions is changed by another. First, she burns with desire for Mandras, but soon her passion ceases, being replaced by an ardent wish to understand the world of politicians, how history unfolds, and the secret study of medicine.

Pelagia's renunciation of her passion for Mandras represents a new stage in the development of our heroine, which is that of a second descent into the underworld, this stage being named by Murdock as "Roads of Trials: Meeting Ogres and Dragons". During this phase, the heroine's endurance against such external dragons as societal norms, conventions, patriarchy, or the inner dragons, such as indecisiveness, fear, and self-doubt, becomes trialled. The heroine must confront and defeat the dragons that make her deviate from the trajectory of the journey of self-accomplishment. During this trial, the heroine must learn to exert her potential and to establish her authority in her environment.

Annis Pratt calls this stage in the development of the heroine as "Splitting off from Family, Husbands, Lovers". In her opinion, this phase represents less a "turning away from societal norms" than "an acute consciousness of the world of the ego" and "an inward plunge away from patriarchal experience" (Pratt, 1981, p. 139). Although the heroine never performs a physical journey, she separates herself psychologically from her former way of perceiving life, changing her worldview as well as her purpose in life.

Pelagia's split from her fantasies about love, passion, and family life takes place gradually, with Mandras' failure to answer to her letters. The distance in time as well in space makes Pelagia experience a kind of distantiation effect, giving her the possibility of alienating herself from her dreams, and, consequently, to judge rationally her relation with Mandras and consider it as a failure.

Experiencing this "acute consciousness of the world of the ego", Pelagia thinks now of her own priorities, of her true purpose in life. When Mandras returns from the war, she feels nothing except compassion, sympathy, and consideration, feelings that she experiences for any other young man who went to war in order to defend his country and returned in such a deplorable situation. She acknowledges clearly that she does not want to marry him and her rejection of Mandras as a lover or husband has nothing to do with his awful physical condition. Her perception of the world has changed radically, and, although she is still a caring young woman, her sense of caring for others is already revealed solely in terms of medical vocation.

This descent, like all possible descents, proves revelatory to Pelagia, because now her capacities are acknowledged. It is a kind of epiphany when "she realized for the first time, and with a small shock, that she had learned enough from her father over the years to become a doctor herself. If there was such a thing as a doctor who was also a woman" (De Bernières, 1995, p. 161). While helping Drosoula to attend her son Mandras, Pelagia experiences a sense of triumph because she is a caregiver after all, a caregiver not in the realm of private, family life, as she has first wished for, but in the realm of public life, in which she becomes useful in and for her community. Pelagia reveals a totally professional attitude of an accomplished doctor when she

> scrutinized the sorry body, freshly washed, and diagnosed every parasite she had ever encountered in the company of her father. 'On the shoulder it's favus. You see, it smells of mice. You need sulphur and salicylic acid for that. It's a kind of honeycomb ringworm. It's lucky it didn't get into the hair, because he would have lost it. These red punctures are body lice. We've got to burn all his clothes, and we've got to shave him all over (…) to get the eggs off his hairs. Or we can wash him in vinegar. And we cover him with eucalyptus oil and paraffin emulsion. The rashes on his legs and arms are bêtes rouges, and we can get rid of them with ammonia and zinc ointment. (…) This patch is pityriasis, you see, it's coffee-coloured. The things we use for the other troubles will cure that too. If you shave him, you know, down there, it'll get rid of any crab lice. (…) And he's got terrible eczema on his arms and calves. We'll have to paint the cracks with iodine, if I can find any, and they'll heal up, and then we just cover him with calamine lotion (…) until it's cured. It might take weeks. We could use olive oil, I suppose, but not in the groin. You shouldn't put anything greasy in the groin. And these maroon prickmarks are flea bites'. (De Bernières, 1995, pp. 165–166)

The practice of medicine fascinates Pelagia; it becomes something like an initiatory journey into wholeness. She feels that her accomplishment liberates her from her inner dragons of self-doubt and former dependencies. However, simultaneously with this satisfaction, Pelagia's inner war goes on, because of the external dragons tearing off her from within. Being a woman and a doctor at the same time increases her sense of inadequacy, feeling an "uncomfortable sensation of having been borne into the wrong world" (De Bernières, 1995, p. 161).

She must confront these external dragons represented by societal norms and conventions of a patriarchal community, which claim that she must marry her fiancé. Her fear of ending her relation with Mandras explicitly stems from these conventions which accept a woman only as someone's wife, as well from her fear of hurting Drosoula, Mandras' mother, for whom Pelagia has developed a great affection.

It is extremely important for the heroine to be able to continue her journey of self-discovery without being intimidated by the sense of her inadequacy. In her desire of self-assertion, the support and encouragement from friends and mentors have a decisive role. In this respect, Drosoula's appreciation of Pelagia has a considerable weight, especially when she understands that Pelagia has detached herself from her son or any idea of marriage, instead "blooming with that peculiar beauty that derives from a sudden sense of vocation" (De Bernières, 1995, p. 167). Drosoula does not hesitate to express her admiration, saying: "Koritsimou, (…) you are the first woman I have ever known who knows anything. Give me a hug" (De Bernières, 1995, p. 166).

Such great support and admiration coming from Drosoula help Pelagia understand who she truly is outside the patriarchal expectations of what she is supposed to be. As Janice Raymond considers, "female friendship helps create the woman of woman's own inventiveness" (Raymond, 2001, p. 5). Drosoula admits Pelagia's uniqueness and this fact encourages Pelagia to explore how she fits in this world of conventions by connecting to other women's experience, women that have also tried to adapt to the same social norms.

Pelagia's father, Dr Iannis, also plays a crucial role in Pelagia's intellectual development. He is the one who encourages his daughter to reject those attitudes and values that do not fit her. In this way, he is the one that stimulates Pelagia to take up the route of finding who she truly is. He is among the first people who have remarked his daughter's uniqueness and tried to cultivate it secretly. When he discovers how Pelagia has attained to her first patient, he could express nothing except admiration: "If I could cook (…) I would have exchange jobs with you. In fact, I may retire. Well done, koritsimou, I have never been so prodigiously proud" (De Bernières, 1995, p. 167).

The acceptance of Pelagia as a doctor by her father, who represents the patriarchy and is the one who directs social norms, becomes a great achievement, because she feels extreme confidence in that now she can truly confront anything in her world. As Murdock notices, "women who have felt accepted by their fathers have confidence that they will be accepted by the world" (Murdock, 1990, p. 31).

Pelagia needs great courage to refuse the identification with the patriarchal image of womanhood and to express her desire of self-assertion. With all the support coming from Drosoula and her father, she still fears isolation and loneliness. Carol S. Pearson claims that "the transformative act for a woman, then, can be seeking her own good and advancement" while "facing her terror of being alone" (Pearson, 1991, p. 262). But in order to find her true purpose in life, as well as her own identity, the heroine must assume the risk of becoming self-sufficient and self-reliant. During this process, "painful though [as] it is at times, she develops a capacity for self-reflection, deliberation and initiative" (Murdock, 2005, p. 168).

This is the heroine's "Boon of Success", as Maureen Murdock calls it, that confers incredible self-confidence. When her reliance on herself becomes extremely boosted, Pelagia does not hesitate to admit openly to Corelli her unusual and utmost desire: "I want to be a doctor" (De Bernières, 1995, p. 206). Her courage is admirable especially when considering that she dares to share her ambitions with a man who has invaded her island, her house, and even her private world of illusions.

At first glance, Pelagia's daring might be surprising, especially in the context of the threat that Corelli represents to her at that moment. However, at a closer look, such daring could be considered as a strategy of disguise that many heroines impose in their wish to depart from what Nadya Aisenberg calls "patriarchal protectorate", and their desire to expose themselves psychologically make them feel free from the pressure of societal approval and is considered as a step towards the establishment of their personal autonomy (Aisenberg, 1994, p. 48).

The hypostasis of a doctor, which Pelagia exhibits to Corelli, represents, in archetypal symbolism, the *persona*, which is the first representation of ourselves that we decide to expose to the people around us. As Clarissa Pinkola Estés claims, "persona is a kind of camouflage which lets others know only what we wish them to know about us, and nothing more" (Estés, 1992, p. 95).

Therefore, Pelagia's admittance that she wants to be a doctor implies an asserted autonomy and authority, essential to her in the context of oppression by the fascists, and hides her fear of becoming submissive and dependent again. The position of a doctor helps Pelagia conceal her vulnerability and makes her hope that she will be taken seriously, as a "strong" person, since she has dared to cross the threshold of the male world and now deserves respect and consideration.

The heroines undergoing this journey, at this stage of their development, prefer to assume a rather masculine behaviour, exhibiting a tough, aggressive and competitive conduct, necessary in order to defeat all the obstacles in their social acceptance within a male culture. Pelagia also experiences a transformation which is revealed first in her mistreatment of Antonio Corelli, when making his staying in her house intolerable by using different remarks and mockeries against all Italians, putting the pine marten into his bed, and terrifying him, or refusing him the pleasure of playing with the little girl Lemoni on the grounds of collaboration.

She exposes a rather tough and aggressive face when considering the possibility of poisoning or shooting him. Such behaviour may be considered to be natural in the context of oppression, but it is also important to stress Pelagia's strength and courage in her fight against any forms of oppression and her refusal to be submissive especially to an invader. Her newly discovered capacity and confidence give her sufficient power to resist the oppression. Pelagia's psychological transformation is also revealed in her determination to continue the study of medicine. Whenever she is left alone in the house, she uses the opportunity to explore the world of medicine that fascinates her so much:

> Then she went inside, took down the two volumes of *The Complete and Concise Home Doctor*, opened them out on the table, and guiltlessly read the sections about reproduction, venereal infections, parturition, and the scrotum. She proceeded at random to read about cascarilla, furred tongue, the anus and its disorders, and anxiety. (De Bernières, 1995, p. 212)

However, although Pelagia undergoes an impressive transformation, she still clings to the feminine self, which is persistent in her psyche. Thus, having changed into an extremely rational individual in her attitude towards the external world, she still feels a kind of nostalgia and regret about her failed relation with Mandras. Seeing him going down to swim in the sea, playing with his dolphins, and returning to her house with a wide smile on his face, makes her remember those days of the past that were free of worry and torment, when their only ambition was to form a family and live happily ever after.

But Pelagia sliding into the nostalgic past is interrupted by the awareness that neither she nor Mandras are the same people as in the past. She has different dreams and aspirations now, and Mandras is transformed as well by his new experiences, ambitions, and frustrations.

The change in their worldview is emphasized in the passage that presents Mandras' second departure, when he comes to Pelagia's house to bid farewell. If in the past Mandras would adore Pelagia, seeing her as sacred, now he does not reveal any respect for her. Although she has struggled hard to heal him after the return from the war, exposing a completely professional behaviour and considerable knowledge that have stirred admiration of both Drosoula and Dr Iannis, Mandras does not seem to appreciate her efforts at all. When he claims that he needs Dr Iannis to cure some bad skin on his arm, Pelagia offers her assistance, which is met with rejection. Mandras, imagining that he is extremely witty, claims: "I was hoping to see the organ-grinder rather than the monkey" (De Bernières, 1995, p. 213).

Mandras acknowledges once again Pelagia's superiority over him, but he is not willing to accept it any longer. If in the past he was proud of his unique fiancé, now it becomes unbearable to him to see Pelagia's development into an accomplished doctor, especially when he has failed in all his enterprises. In his frustration, he destroys the beautiful relation that has existed between them in the past.

Although Pelagia's eyes "flashed fire" because of the anger of being rejected so harshly, she finds enough strength to treat him well, since she knows that he will go with the partisans to defend their country. She accepts Mandras' determination to rebel against oppression and in this respect they are both quite alike. Impressed by his courage to revolt even in such a desperate situation, Pelagia wants to give him a token, something important that will make him feel valuable. She wants to make him feel appreciated by a woman who has made something only for him and with such a great effort:

> Pelagia went inside a moment and came out bearing the waistcoat that she had so devotedly made and embroidered whilst her fiancé had been at front. She showed it to him diffidently, saying, 'This is what I was making for you, to dance at feasts. Do you want to take it now?' Mandras took it and held it up. He cocked his head to one side and said, 'It doesn't quite match up, does it? I mean, the pattern is a little different on each side.' Pelagia felt a pang of disappointment that tasted of betrayal. 'I tried so hard', she exclaimed piteously, in a rush of emotion, 'and I can never please you'. (De Bernières, 1995, pp. 213–214)

Pelagia's brutal rejection by Mandras makes her feel frustrated, because her efforts have not been accepted and approved. She experiences once again a sense of inadequacy, because Mandras, the man who once loved and appreciated her greatly, chooses to humiliate her to such a degree. Her being rejected as a doctor within the male environment and her being rejected as a woman performing feminine acts lead her to feel a sense of failure that she has never experienced before. She also feels betrayed by a person who was once mostly loyal to her. These aspects shatter her earlier gained self-confidence, and reduce her as a woman, as well as a human being, and lead her to the awareness that she is alone, a pariah in her community, unable to rely on anybody. This awareness increases her fear of being alone in an already invaded space, and despair and anxiety overwhelm her completely.

This phase of the heroine's journey is named by Maureen Murdock as "Awakening to Feelings of Spiritual Aridity: Death". It is the stage that precedes initiation and develops out of the heroine's forced separation from the feminine and deceptive boon of success. Pelagia's partition from Mandras leaves her with the feeling of aridity, emptiness, and inadequacy. The sense of betrayal that she experiences is not stimulated only by Mandras' behaviour, but also by her own sense of insufficiency, since she has abandoned the Feminine in her quest for her own self, and it turned out to be not only unsatisfactory but above all disappointing. Pelagia experiences a sense of failure, because she has made a wrong choice while following her desires and now she is alone, vulnerable, and afraid to disappoint her father.

The traditional hero performs the return after the physical, outward movement, whereas the heroine's journey is defined by the spiritual, inward movement into the Self. The heroine, following the trajectory of her spiritual and psychological transformation, becomes arid, sterile, and reaches the acceptance of the authority of the unconscious over the conscious mind. The heroine's quest is not thus defined by "conquest and domination; it is a quest to bring balance into our lives through the marriage of both feminine and masculine aspects of our nature" (Murdock, 1990, p. 129).

But in order to succeed in this enterprise, the heroine must explore this *terra incognita* of her unconscious by choosing, again, between the unfolding paths. This moment of changing paths implies the abandonment of the one that the heroine has already travelled by, and the crossing of some other thresholds which are full of new obstacles and dangers, yet without any assurance that the new path will lead to success and fulfilment.

This phase, called by Murdock as "Initiation and Descent to the Goddess", often reveals the heroine's loss of self-confidence and the acquiring of misfortune, grief, depression, and alienation. However, although the heroine undergoing this stage in her quest may be regarded by the members of her family and community as unstable or depressed, one should consider, as Meredith Powers does, the healing and renewing aspects of initiation and descent: "The descents, so long misunderstood by patriarchal exegesis, are clearly made in the service of life. As I see it, it is in this that the archetypal heroine gains her sustaining strength" (Powers, 1991, p. 154).

Maureen Murdock continues this line of idea, and specifies that although the descent and the feminine cycle can be terrifying and painful, "if we have the patience to allow the process its full due, deep healing can occur. If we abort our process we never allow ourselves to come to full term" (Murdock, 1990, p. 108).

Pelagia provides a relevant example of the healing power by communing with the wild feminine, though her process is a long and gradual one. Now, when she feels alone and experiences a sense of failure, she is looking for a new path which she could explore in order to find out who she really is. It is in this crucial moment of her existence that she receives the necessary support which comes unexpectedly from the one who has invaded her world, that is, from Antonio Corelli.

Symbolically, by sharing the same space, which is Pelagia's house, Antonio manages to investigate this familiar to Pelagia place and bring to light those aspects of it that still remain unexplored or ignored. In this house, Antonio discovers an unknown aspect of Pelagia's life, which is her artistic talent that gives her a chance to develop a unique self. In the kitchen, Antonio notices the "exquisitely embroidered waistcoat" that has been earlier rejected brutally by Mandras. Antonio

> picked it up and held it against the light; the velvet was richly scarlet, and the satin lining was sewn in with tiny conscientious threads that looked as though they could only have been done by the fingers of a diminutive sylph. In gold and yellow thread he saw languid flowers, soaring eagles and leaping fish. He ran his finger over the embroidery and felt the density of the designs. He closed his eyes and realized that each figure recapitulated in relief the curves of the creature it portrayed. (De Bernières, 1995, p. 215)

This discovery has a tremendous impact upon Pelagia, because she has the opportunity to heal herself from the sense of failure and inadequacy that has overwhelmed her in the past. It is difficult for her to escape her own frustrations; when she discovers the waistcoat in Antonio's hands, she feels again ashamed and inadequate. She is embarrassed especially by remembering the imperfections noticed earlier by Mandras, because to her, these imperfections may reveal her lack of abilities that she has believed to possess and has trusted. Although reduced by her shame, Pelagia confronts Antonio, admitting openly her failure:

> I made it. And it's not so good. (…) It doesn't match up properly on both sides. They are supposed to be mirror images of each other, and if you look, this eagle is at a different angle to that one, and this flower is supposed to be the same size as that one, but it's bigger. (De Bernières, 1995, p. 215)

Antonio assumes the role of a guide for Pelagia, since he acknowledges that even in her domestic and feminine acts, she, unconsciously, tends to assert her uniqueness. In his attempt to encourage and support Pelagia in her exceptionality, he explains:

> Symmetry is only a property of dead things. Did you ever see a tree or a mountain that was symmetrical? It's fine for buildings, but if you ever see a symmetrical human face, you will have the impression that you ought to think it beautiful, but that in fact you find it cold. The human heart likes a little disorder in its geometry, Kyria Pelagia. Look at your face in a mirror, Signorina, and you will see that one eyebrow is a little higher than the other, that the set of the lid of your left eye is a fraction more open than

the other. It is these things that make you both attractive and beautiful, whereas ... otherwise you would be a statue. (De Bernières, 1995, p. 215)

Everything that has been earlier seen by Pelagia as negative or failed aspects of her own self, is now revised by her through Antonio's contribution. The renewal of these neglected and relegated aspects helps her re-evaluate herself and abandon the insecurities that have tormented her in the past. When Antonio offers money to buy the waistcoat, which is to him a masterpiece, Pelagia refuses to sell it, because this waistcoat becomes a symbol of her worth as well as a sign of her reconnection with the feminine aspects within herself. Pelagia reinvents herself, in different terms this time, by reuniting with the "dark feminine" archetypal images that were earlier abandoned by her.

This stage of the journey, called by Maureen Murdock as "Urgent Yearning to Reconnect with the Feminine", reveals the heroine's ardent wish to regain the neglected feminine aspects of her own self. She illustrates a "desire to develop those parts of herself that have gone underground while on the heroic quest: her body, her emotions, her spirit, her creative wisdom" (Murdock, 1990, p. 111).

Sewing, weaving, spinning, crocheting, and embroidering have always been powerful metaphors of femininity. These kinds of activities do not just reveal the creative aspects of the heroines; they, as Bettina Knapp claims, "refine and shape what is considered crude, unaesthetic, and unserviceable. As such, they may also be viewed as transformation rituals" (Knapp, 1997, p. 161). By these activities, the heroines reveal their uniqueness and worth in the world. It is interesting to mention here the reference that Michael Meade makes with regard to this metaphor, namely the story of an old woman weaving a tapestry while sitting in a cave (Meade, 2009, Lecture). Each time she goes to mix the stew, her tapestry is unravelled by a black dog. The old woman never scolds the dog, but sits calmly in her place and weaves the tapestry anew, making it more and more beautiful each time. According to Meade, the tapestry of the old woman represents the metaphor of life, a continuous process of making-unmaking-making anew. This story reminds of a similar motif of the Three Fates from a Greek myth in which three old women spin out and cut the lives of people. Another allusion is to Penelope's unravelling of her tapestry every night in order to delay the confrontation with the suitors. Also, the Greek goddess Athena is a deity representing war as well as weaving, to which Neith, an Egyptian goddess, may be added as representing the same attributes associated with devastation and remaking.

For Pelagia, the moment of the discovery of the waistcoat's value functions as a revelation of her connection with the feminine and as the beginning of her apprenticeship – or rather the re-apprenticeship – in the realm of feminine power.

Her constant weaving of the coverlet and its unravelling represent her newly gained power and knowledge necessary for the building and rebuilding of her own life, as well the reinvention of her own self. She tangles Corelli by her threads, holding complete control over his feelings. She weaves the tapestry of her life with him and every time she wishes to change something in it, she has the power to make it anew. Most powerfully, this metaphor of sewing is revealed when Dr Iannis and Pelagia operate Antonio after the massacre. As if Pelagia's powers are extended upon life and death,

> she was stitching up her lover with an accuracy and care that she owed to an asymmetrical waistcoat and the patient instruction of an aunt, and there was her father next to her, carefully extracting splinters of rib and flattened bullets from the same man's chest (…). (De Bernières, 1995, pp. 413–414)

We do not have again that cold, rational and detached attitude which she revealed when healing Mandras after his homecoming. She is not acting only as a doctor now. This time, she is attending Antonio carefully and professionally, but her professionalism reminds us mostly of an artistic or creative act. Moreover, the decision about the way in which to re-create Antonio's appearance is solely hers. She reminds us of the powers of the goddess Aruru from the Mesopotamian mythology, who creates man and infuses life into him; or rather of the goddess Isis who restores the body of Osiris, her husband, after his murder. Definitely, Pelagia possesses the power of a goddess when

> she moved to the captain's face and cleaned out the bullet crease. She wandered to let it heal on its own or whether to sew it up. 'It depends.' Said the doctor, (…) 'whether you want him with a crooked smile or not. It's a choice between that or a wide scar. Either of them may be charming, who knows?' 'A scar can be romantic.' said Pelagia. (De Bernières, 1995, p. 414)

Corelli's body is cut and sewn in an almost ritualistic manner, where Pelagia displays power and authority by using feminine ways of knowledge. Her decision concerning the scar on his face is done in a unique, feminine way that has nothing to do with reason. Her choice of leaving the scar without sewing it is based on her feelings, since she considers that Antonio will look more romantic in this way.

Pelagia's learning to use her judgment reflects Jung's concept of transcendent function, which is the mediating force between two polarized tendencies within the psyche. The transcendent function stems out of intense and concentrated tensions within the individual. These extreme and excruciating oppositions provide the possibility for the individual to transcend the ego boundaries and attain a perception of reality which is no longer divided into two conflicting forces. Jung considers that it is essential to hold the balance between these opposites in order to make the link between ego-consciousness and the unconscious.

Pelagia's reliance on her feelings and sensibility in taking decisions and her trust of her own judgment represent symbolically her capacity of including both feminine and masculine elements within her psyche, which leads to the accomplishment of her personality.

Another way of reconnecting with the feminine in the case of Pelagia, as in the case of many other heroines, takes place through the discovery of her own intuition. Although intuition for Pelagia has always been a mode to know the truth, she has scarcely been aware of its reliability. Very early in her relation with Mandras, Pelagia's inner voice dictated the truth:

> She thought about war and felt her heart grow heavy, reflecting that in the old days men were the playthings of gods, and had advanced no further than to become the toys of other men who thought that they themselves were gods. She played with the euphony of words; 'Hitler, Attila, Caligula. Hitler, Attila, Caligula.' She found no word to accompany 'Mussolini' until she came up with 'Metaxas'. 'Mussolini, Metaxas', she said, and added, 'Mandras'. (De Bernières, 1995, pp. 104–105)

She did not know at that time how to trust her inner voice, and relied, instead, on her reason, and dismissed immediately the idea of Mandras' possible connection to any of these dictators, claiming that he is "too much without malice" (De Bernières, 1995, p. 105).

As Clarissa Pinkola Estés explains, "this great power, intuition, is composed of lightning-fast inner seeing, inner hearing, inner-sensing, and inner knowing" (Estés, 1992, p. 80). Possessing a split between reason and intuition, Pelagia still does not know how to trust her inner voice. It is due to Antonio Corelli's intervention, who becomes Pelagia's mentor in the realm of sensibility by the power of music, which provides her with the possibility to use her power wisely and make the right choice. Her falling in love with Corelli is against any rules of reason, because he represents fascism and is an invader of her country, her island and her house.

However, Pelagia eventually learns to rely on her intuition or inner voice, admits her feelings and then objectifies them, providing them with significance and a proper consideration. Her love for Corelli is not a blind passion. On the contrary, she gives him worth as a human being who behaves honestly, who never enjoys any bloodshed or aggression, who defends justice, and who is an officer in the fascist army only due to the wrong course of events. Also, Pelagia values Antonio greatly for his exceptional talent, extraordinary capacity of playing mandolin, as well as for his unique way of using music as a bridging force that covers the huge gap between the locals and Italians. By learning to trust her intuition and objectifying the knowledge gained by it, Pelagia makes the right choice and discovers the love of her life: Antonio Corelli, her animus, in Jungian terms.

Tilmann Betsch describes intuition in the following terms:

> Intuition is a process of thinking. The input to this process is mostly provided by knowledge stored in long-term memory that has been primarily acquired via associative learning. The input is processed automatically and without conscious awareness. The output of the process is a feeling that can serve as a basis for judgment and decisions. (Betsch, 2008, p. 4)

Similarly, Pelagia's newly acquired power teaches her not to reflect upon a problem reasonably and logically, but to trust her prior experiences which are also important and valuable sources of knowledge. Above all, she learns to gain knowledge through her feelings and intuition, but she also discovers to be objective when relying on them.

This is, actually, her great achievement that contributes to her self-development. However, though Pelagia gains such a unique wisdom, it does not prevent her from subsequent affliction. Antonio's departure causes her tremendous suffering, for he is leaving the island in a very turbulent moment and with a precarious health. The uncertainty about his survival and the uncertainty concerning his love and an eventual return to her become the source of Pelagia's constant torment. Moreover, the Nazis' abuse and crimes against the people on the island, including Pelagia and her father, leave her deeply wounded and affected. The Liberation, which they have desperately expected to occur, brings to them another wave of pain, rape, and cruelty that seem again to be endless. Having no strength to grieve,

> alone in the house, penniless and helpless, stricken by a second dose of inconsolable despair, she thought for the first time in her life of ending everything by suicide. She saw no future except the succession of one type of Fascism by another, on an island seemingly accursed and destined forever to be a part of someone else's game, a game whose cynical players changed but whose counters were fashioned out of bone and blood, the flesh of all the innocent and weak. (De Bernières, 1995, p. 444)

Like Albert Camus' Sisyphus, who is conscious of the extent of his own misery and aware of his absurd existence, reflecting whether suicide is a legitimate solution out of this desperate existence, Pelagia, in her anxiety, is also aware of her condition and tries to find an answer to this question. When her hope has been exhausted in vain in this indifferent universe, she tries desperately to connect herself to a nation, to people living a meaningful and worthy life. But this attempt fails as well:

The Nazis had slaughtered 60,000 Greek Jews, (...) and now her own people killed their brothers as if the Nazis had only been a police force whose departure had been eagerly awaited by the fratricides. She heard that the Communists had been killing off the Italian soldiers who had come to fight alongside them against the Germans. She remembered the happy boys of La Scala, she remembered saying that she would always hate the Nazis. Had the time come, finally, to always hate the Greeks? Of the nations who had broken into her house to beat her and steal her possessions, only the Italians were innocent, it seemed. She thought of how the British were too slow to come (...). And if she hated the Greeks, to which people did she now belong? She was without father, without possessions, without food, without love, without hope, without country. (De Bernières, 1995, pp. 444–445)

The confrontation of the illogical and longing heart of Pelagia with the indifferent world brings her to experience the absurd. But although embittered and depressed, and finding herself at the bottom of the mountain every time she attempts to climb it, a true heroine must learn throughout the quest to survive the despair that overwhelms her. In order to complete her journey, Pelagia must continue to exist and must learn to overcome loss, grief, and anxiety.

This period of depression can be again symbolically associated with the underworld or labyrinthine passages from various myths, out of which the heroine must emerge to light. This period represents the heroine's battles, her agony between life and death. It represents also a kind of ritual of transformation, since the one that survives the infernal experiences emerges, eventually, radically transformed.

Pelagia manages to transcend the infernal experiences by the help of Drosoula, Mandras' mother. In this respect, Pearson and Pope insist upon the role of a supportive mother as a congenial parental figure in this stage of the heroine's journey:

> Usually, when the hero is at the nadir of despair, a nurturing, strong, and independent woman appears to her (...). The powerful and heroic woman whom she encounters may be a surrogate mother figure. Unlike the male seducer who claims that he can slay the dragons for her, the female rescue figure tells the hero that she is capable of saving herself. (Pearson and Pope, 1981, pp. 184–185)

Drosoula replaces the actual mother whom Pelagia has never known. Although Drosoula knows that Pelagia's love for Mandras has dissipated away as a result of his long absence and long silence, and more recently his inadequate character, she comes to love Pelagia as her own daughter, accepting even the fact that the young woman is desperately in love with the Italian captain and is waiting for his return. In the most crucial moment of Pelagia's desolation, Drosoula knows how to support and protect her. For Pelagia's safety, Drosoula moves to the doctor's house and offers all the compassion and sustenance that she is capable of:

> For comfort they slept together in doctor's bed, and by day they concocted schemes to find supplies of food and listened to each other's plaints and tales. They dug for roots in the maquis, sprouted ancient beans in dishes, lethally disturbed the hibernation of hedgehogs, and Drosoula took her young friend down the rocks to learn to fish and turn the stones for crabs, returning with seaweed to serve in place of vegetables and salt. (De Bernières, 1995, p. 445)

This image of the two women digging for roots, cultivating beans, catching crabs, and entering the water for fish and seaweed, resembles the motif of the descent into the underworld, a necessary part in the heroine's journey, and only the wisdom and skills of the heroine represent a means of escaping the underworld. Frequently, myths revealing the motif of the descent of the heroine, include the phase of the heroine's encounter with a hag, or a witch, or even death, which forces the heroine to confront the enemy, and, as a result of this confrontation, the heroine is given valuable advice or knowledge of how to avoid the snares of the underworld and how to get out to light.

Clarissa Pinkola Estés, who has vastly examined the feminine archetypes in various fairy tales and folk literature, notices the cyclical nature of the heroine's journey, which she calls as "Life/Death/Life" cycle (Estés, 1992). She claims that although death is destructive in this cycle, it has a strong, positive aspect, since it confers the possibility of life renewal. As Estés suggests, the image of the Lady Death has a curative and creative property, which has been preserved in various personifications of the Goddess. By the fearless confrontation of the Death aspect of women, people acquire the awareness that death and other loses are part of life. Only when accepting consciously the death or the loss of someone, or the end of illusions or expectations, one becomes able to continue his or her life, and, eventually, encounter love.

This is also to be observed in each of Pelagia's infernal experiences of descent, each ending in a new awareness of her capacities.

The old Drosoula, symbolically, represents the Lady Death, her physical appearance being extremely suggestive in this respect:

> Her great ugly moon of a face had shrunk inwards, giving her an air of ethereal soulfulness despite her thick lips and massive brows. Her cheerful rolls of fat had fallen from her thighs and hips, and the massive promontory of her maternal bosom had lapsed downwards into the space left vacant by the erstwhile exuberance of her stomach. Arthritis had begun to afflict one knee and both joints of the thigh, and she walked now with a slow dragging and jerking motion that was painful and mechanical to behold. Her new and unwanted slenderness lent dignity to her height, however, and her grey hairs inspired respect and left her more formidable. (De Bernières, 1995, p. 445)

Fearful, like an old crone, Drosoula, however, is extremely intelligent, strong, and affectionate; in her ferocious manner, she desperately protects Pelagia. As we are told in the novel, "her spirit was unbroken, and she gave Pelagia strength" (De Bernières, 1995, p. 445). This old and unfortunate woman is "both friend and mother to all those who have lost their way, all those who need learning, all those who have a riddle to solve, all those out in the forest or the desert wandering and searching" (Estés, 1992, p. 8). Without her instructions and support, Pelagia would not have managed to get through her deplorable situation and to learn to evaluate life again. Without Drosoula's help, Pelagia would not have found the way out of the darkness of the underworld; and, without Drosoula, Pelagia would not have achieved a greater understanding of death. As Death preserves the feminine ability to transform, Drosoula possesses a transformative power, through wielding life and death, and, by making a tremendous impact upon Pelagia, the young woman gains the necessary wisdom to sustain her life and to continue her journey.

Pelagia's transformation becomes a kind of resurrection, a return from death to life, which facilitates her transition into the next stage of her quest. Maureen Murdock calls this moment in the heroine's journey as "Healing the Mother/Daughter Split", a phase which involves the healing of the fracture of the feminine nature in general. During this stage, the heroine regains the lost voice through the communion with other women. Pelagia's split is cured by Drosoula's help, as well as by the appearance of Antonia, a newly born girl that has been abandoned in front of Pelagia's house and that has filled the two women's emptiness, providing a purpose for their existence:

> The two women, whose souls had been so continuously tempered in the crucibles of bereavement and unhappiness, found in Antonia a new and poignant focus for their lives. There was no penury too grievous to endure that she did not make sufferable, no tragic memory that she could not efface, and she took her place in that providential matriarchy as though designed for it by fate. (De Bernières, 1995, pp. 454–455)

Drosoula fulfils her dream of having a daughter and Pelagia is able to accomplish her desire of becoming a mother, offering guidance, assistance, and nurturance within the family web. Pelagia's perpetual thirst for caring and assisting the others is satisfied by Antonia's existence, a fact which prevents Pelagia's decay into despair again, especially when she has been refused the right of practicing medicine. Deprived of the possibility to practice medicine, and, in this way, deprived of any possibility to have an income, Pelagia feels herself a misfit, swayed by social pressure. Acknowledging her difference from other women in their community, living and running the house in an unconventional way, Pelagia and the two other women in her house create a kind of matriarchal aegis, being perceived as outcasts by the entire community:

Eccentric they were seen to be. The empty-headed gossips of the village transformed Drosoula, with her extreme ugliness, and Pelagia with her fearless lack of deference to men, into a pair of harridans and witches. The fact that the doctor was silent and impotent in the house was explained away by means of chemically emasculating potions and ottoman spells, and the fact that Pelagia was driven by impecuniousness to resort to valerian and thyme rather than to sophisticated modern drugs merely served to exacerbate the certainty that their methods were suspicious and occult. Children stoned them as they passed, taunting them, and adults warned their children to keep away and encouraged their dogs to bite them. (De Bernières, 1995, pp. 457–458)

But this isolation does not damage Pelagia. On the contrary, by defying the communal conventions and remaining cut off from the rest of the people, our heroine gains the possibility to develop an inner world in which she can be true to herself. Pelagia discovers a realm to dwell, where she will be close to the feminine nature. By exploring new spaces and new possibilities, which represent, symbolically, new facets of her psyche, Pelagia is searching for other, uncultivated by her so far possibilities for personal development. Reawakening some forgotten yearnings or some abandoned aspirations, she reclaims the lost authority which is necessary for her self-assertion.

Although Pelagia's reawakening is a gradual and slow process, she reclaims her inner power which has been erased from her by the patriarchal culture. During this recovery process, she chooses celibacy and asexuality, because she thinks that Antonio is dead and there could be no one worthy to replace him. Prior to her learning process about the connection with the others, the heroine experiences the need for loneliness, a time that may help her, as Annis Pratt claims, "to pass through and beyond Eros (…) thus, to achieve selfhood through a creative solitude" (Pratt, 1981, p. 127).

For Pelagia, this period of isolation provides an opportunity for self-reflection, which is essential in her attempt to deal with her low-esteem caused by her being rejected by the community. Above all, this phase of solitude is beneficial in the process of discovery of her own self. As Pratt specifies, the heroine demands a time in seclusion in order to surpass "the difficulty of creating a life for herself when she has belonged to someone else for years" (Pratt, 1981, p. 129).

Pelagia's rebirth begins, ironically, with an earthquake. The earth was shattered literally, the natural calamity smashing away the old house and the entire village, as well as her inner world. The mytheme of Orpheus and Eurydice has been inverted here, Pelagia representing Orpheus and Dr Iannis, lost in the womb of the earth, representing Eurydice.

In our opinion, the comparison with Orpheus is justified by the extreme creative abilities and powers acquired by the heroine only after the loss of a precious person. Pelagia loses her father during the earthquake, and this experience devastates her emotionally. Pelagia is again destroyed psychologically and spiritually, because she feels guilty for failing to save her father's life during the calamity. She collapses into another depression caused by her sense of guilt, decaying more and more into the abyss. But, as Pelagia has learned the cyclical nature of life and has gained the knowledge of death, she discovers enough strength within herself as to regenerate and create something new and original.

This strength, as in the earlier periods of crisis, has been fused by the wisdom and ingenuity of Drosoula. Relying on Pelagia's excessive love for her father, Drosoula encourages the young woman to finish her father's project of writing history, and in this way to keep the memory of Dr Iannis alive. Pelagia's reawakening suggests her resurrection; from her own ashes she struggles for life through the writing of history, a creative aspect uncultivated by her so far:

> It was surprisingly easy. She has read through the manuscripts so many times that all the old phrases rolled through the kitchen door and windows, made themselves heard inaudibly, and flowed down her arm and right hand, emerging from the nib of her pen and filling sheet after sheet of paper: 'The half-forgotten island of Cephallonia rises improvidently and inadvisedly from the Ionian Sea; it is an island so immense in antiquity that the very rocks themselves exhale nostalgia and the red earth is stupefied not only by the sun, but by the impossible weight of memory (…)'. (De Bernières, 1995, p. 485)

The writing of history, in the case of Pelagia, as in the case of many other women, reminds of a journey of self-understanding, during which the earlier explored purposes, like relationships with other people, are being revived, but these priorities become "increasingly secondary, giving way to a puzzling over the nature of the cosmos itself rather than over human entanglements" (Pratt, 1981, p. 129).

Pelagia's time of seclusion from the social demands proves to be prolific; her perception broadens, crosses the family and social boundaries, and the heroine achieves a new and more objective sense of abstract ideal, unknown to her so far. She has discovered a strange and mysterious delight in writing, an activity that has stimulated her renewal:

> The joy of it transformed her. Her act of filial devotion metamorphosed into a grand design involving trips to the library and earnest letters of enquiry to learned institutions, to maritime museums, the British Library, experts on Napoleon, and American Professors of the history of Imperial Power. To her amazement and gratification she discovered that all over the world there were enthusiastic people so enamoured with knowledge and its coherent explanation that they would actually spend months making enquiries on her behalf, and eventually send her much more that she had asked for, with personal notes of encouragement and lists of other experts and institutions to consult. As the piles of correspondence mounted, she began to feel in danger of

finishing up by writing a 'Universal History of the Entire World', because everything connected to everything else in the most elaborate, devious and elegant ways. (De Bernières, 1995, p. 486)

The experience of writing history represents one of the most important phases of return in Pelagia's journey, which is called by Maureen Murdock as "Healing the Wounded Masculine"; it requires the heroine's discovery and acceptance of all aspects of herself. This acceptance refers to freeing oneself from "machisma", "warrior" archetype, and the recognition of all those aspects of the self that have remained repressed. As Murdock asserts, for the heroine, "the challenge is not one of conquest but one of acceptance, of accepting her nameless, unloved parts that have become tyrannical because she has left them unchecked" (Murdock, 1990, p. 158). In order to bring out "The Inner Man with Heart", as Murdock terms it, the heroine must permit the masculine and feminine creative energies to adjust and complement one another through the unification of opposite qualities, leading to the "Sacred Marriage". As the critic further explains, the heroine experiences "sacred marriage" when she "comes to understand the dynamics of her feminine and masculine nature and accepts them both together", by which attaining "the marriage of ego and the self" (Murdock, 1990, p. 160).

Pelagia manages to balance and integrate both feminine and masculine creative energies within herself, and she becomes able to accept her "nameless, unloved parts", which in the novel are suggested by the historical writings of her father, unappreciated by Pelagia earlier, since she has become disillusioned by her "great" nation and disappointed by the course of history in general. However, she finds sufficient strength and wisdom to go beyond her damaging attitude, especially due to great admiration and respect that she feels for her father, and, by balancing the creative energies, Pelagia accomplishes successfully her task. The integration of the masculine and feminine creative energies is presented in the novel in an extremely ingenious manner:

> Pelagia almost became the doctor. As in the time of her distress, and just as he had done throughout his life, she did virtually nothing about the house, leaving it all to the women. Of the few souvenirs of her father, dug from the ruins, there remained his pipe, and this she stuck between her teeth as he had done, inhaling the traces of tarry dottle, and impressing the stem with the indentations of her own teeth over the marks of his. She did not light it, but regarded it as an instrument of her mediumship, so that the old words now seemed to flow in through the empty bowl, gather in the stem, and sound directly in her brain. Tentatively she began to add a woman's touch to the male prepossessions of the text, supplying details of manners of dress and the techniques of baking in the communal fourno, the economic significance of child labour, and the cruel but traditional contempt for widows. (De Bernières, 1995, pp. 485–486)

This moment represents, in archetypal terms, the encounter with the father, when the young hero or heroine attains the atonement and the approval of the paternal figure, which are necessary in the journey of self-accomplishment. For Pelagia, however, this occasion serves to consummate all the psychological differences that existed between father and daughter during their life. But at this stage of her development, though she imitates the physical behaviour of her father, she does not identify with him any longer.

On the contrary, Pelagia has achieved a stage in her self-development in which she can freely express her ideas, without fearing to be chastised by others; she has developed enough self-esteem and confidence to argue and challenge her father's point of view: "As she wrote, she discovered her own passions whose existence she had never previously suspected, and out onto the page there soared thundering condemnations and acid verdicts to rival and outvenom his" (De Bernières, 1995, p. 486).

Although Pelagia has admired her father and experienced immense esteem for him throughout her life, she is not willing to identify with him anymore. This aspect represents a great success in the development of her personality and in the attainment of the self.

She develops a wider vision of the world, and she can integrate in the society again and reconnect with it without any fears. Through deep meditation and pensiveness, Pelagia develops her own perception of life, a perception that allows her to act freely, out of conviction or love, leaving behind the earlier yearnings of the ego and the desolated sense of duty that so far has prevented her from self-accomplishment. By developing such an attitude, Pelagia is able to confront any situation that life or community might create in her path.

As a result, when she dares to return to society and form relationships with many other intellectuals through correspondence, getting their approval and encouragement, Pelagia feels elevated, experiencing the delight of attaining the boon, "her intellectual baby", her history. She reveals enormous courage in offering it for publication, and even more strength when it is rejected on the grounds of having no market. Nevertheless, Pelagia's newly acquired perception of the world does not permit her to yield, because now she is able to make the difference between what she was before writing the history and what she has become now:

> The calligraphy near the beginning was as spidery and unhinged as that of her father during the long years of his silence, but as time progressed it had become firmer and more rounded, more confident and affirmative. But more importantly than this, the process of writing has crystallised opinions and philosophical positions that she had not even known that she had held. She discovered that her basic understanding of

economic process was Marxist, but that, paradoxically, she thought that capitalism had the best ways of dealing with the problems. She considered that cultural traditions were a stronger force in history than economic transformations, and that human nature was fundamentally irrational to the point of insanity, which accounted for its demagoguery and unbelievable beliefs, and she concluded that freedom and order were not mutually exclusive, but essential preconditions of each other. (De Bernières, 1995, p. 487)

Pelagia is no longer looking for social acceptance or approval. She grows to the awareness that writing history signifies the creation of her own self, because only now she can develop to such a degree that she is able to cultivate her own voice, to speak up openly, even publicly, asserting her right to express her own opinions and points of view, and to come to confront life from her own premises. She can neither be intimidated by social rejection nor can she be reduced as a human being, because now she has learned to act in response.

Through her newly attained perception of the world, through imagination and creativity, Pelagia stands for herself, and, though rejected by publishers, her creative power is, indirectly, nurturing for her community. As Clarissa Pinkola Estés claims,

> creativity is not a solitary movement. That is its power. Whatever is touched by it, whoever hears it, senses it, knows it, is fed (…). A single creative act has the potential to feed a continent. One creative act can cause a torrent to break through stone. For this reason, a woman's creative ability is her most valuable asset. (Estés, 1992, p. 299)

Pelagia will leave a legacy to her world, which is her history that she will donate after her death. The value of this history is to be evaluated by the posterity, since it is written by a "substantial intellectual in the great Hellenic tradition" (De Bernières, 1995, p. 487). Pelagia reveals herself to the community through her creative work, but she does not want any social reward. The only reward that she needs is on the private level, since she is still searching for personal accomplishment. There is one more frustration that overshadows the sense of victory, causing regret and damaging her self-esteem: her insufficiency as a woman who has never given birth to a baby.

However, Pelagia has gained sufficient wisdom to understand that, though she cannot give birth, Antonia, her daughter, is able to give this reward. Pelagia has also grown to the awareness that she may become a good role model for celebrating the feminine qualities, and she has the potential to nurture without any damage to the development of the baby.

Antonia refuses vehemently the idea of giving birth, claiming that "It's my body (…) and it's not fair to expect me to be constrained by an accident of biology. (…)

Anyway, the world's already overpopulated, and it's my right to have a choice" (De Bernières, 1995, p. 493). However, although Pelagia is insistent at first, she reveals enough judgment and patience to wait for Antonia's own awareness of the importance for a woman to give birth. She proves discernment by refusing to impose with despotism and authority her will upon Antonia; instead, she awaits quietly Antonia's coming of age. The little boy that came to life represents her greatest toffee:

> Pelagia cradled the infant in her arms, feeling all the sadness of a woman who has remained a virgin and technically childless all her life, and began to refer to it as Iannis. She referred to it so often by that name that it soon seemed obvious to its parents that it could not be Kyriakos or Vassos or Stratis or Dionisos. If you called it Iannis, it smiled and blew slimy bubbles that burst and trickled down its chin, and so Iannis it was. (De Bernières, 1995, pp. 495–496)

Pelagia's regrets and sorrows dissipate in the presence of this baby, whom she names Iannis, and understands that this is the greatest reward that a woman may receive throughout her quest for the self. Despite her various accomplishments and a strong sense of self-fulfilment, she acknowledges that no social award or achievement can ever compensate or replace the miracle and the power of heredity. This is one of the most valuable legacies that a woman leaves to the world. Through the birth of little Iannis, Pelagia reclaims her discarded femininity and learns to balance and integrate both feminine and masculine creative energies, attaining her final sense of self-accomplishment.

The heroine of the monomyth faces now the last stage of her journey, which is called by Maureen Murdock as "Integration of Masculine and Feminine". During this last part of the quest, the heroine attains the harmonious equilibrium of feminine and masculine aspects of the self, conceiving the ultimate sense of wholeness and accomplished selfhood. The beneficial outcome of this harmonious integration of masculine and feminine energies, when attained at the individual level, should contribute to the "change the consciousness on the planet from one of addiction to suffering, conflict, and domination, to a consciousness that recognizes the need for affiliation, healing, balance and *inter-being*" (Murdock, 1990, p. 183).

Pelagia feels almost completely fulfilled with little Iannis by her side, caring for him, teaching him Italian, cultivating in him the love for nature and the universe, and encouraging him to love music. Pelagia has accomplished and left behind the status and role of a caregiver that seeks her identity through relationships within the family web. Pelagia has developed as an individual, her worldview has changed radically, and in her search to develop beyond the boundaries, she does not confine herself any longer to her family net. Her wisdom and love determine her to go beyond the limits, traverse all the boundaries, and care for every person who needs help. As a manager of Drosoula's tavern, Pelagia welcomes tourists from all over the world, representing different cultures, speaking different languages, being of different genders and ages, and having different goals in their life.

And Pelagia cares for them all, connects with them all, and nurtures them all. Her tavern resembles a little microcosm in which the matriarchal goddess reveals her benign face to her world. Through music, nourishment, and love, the Mother Goddess attains a perfect example of human communion and harmony. By healing the fracture caused by suffering, conflict and domination, she brings balance and concord to her world, having as her major goal the collective good. This is actually Pelagia's greatest success in life.

But in order to complete her journey, Pelagia must yet attain a harmoniously balanced self, which becomes possible only when the heroine has lived through her yearnings and desires, abandoning all regrets and the bitterness that have marked her life. Only after some fifty years, when Antonio Corelli shows up his face to Pelagia, her journey and quest are completed.

Corelli was alive all these years and visited the island and Pelagia regularly, but he never revealed his presence and never disclosed his identity to either Pelagia or another person on the island. Misled by Antonia's presence, he would not wish to disturb Pelagia's order of life, preferring instead to observe her incognito. Their first meeting after a too long separation resembles the mythical confrontation of the Mother Goddess and the Sky Father in their battle for supremacy. Pelagia's fury is released upon Antonio, who

> although in his seventies, rediscovered a certain amount of youthful agility in his old limbs. He dodged a cast-iron frying pan, and winced as it smashed the window behind him. "Sporcaccione! Figlio d'un culo!" Pelagia shrieked. "Pezzo di merda! All my life waiting, all my life mourning, all my life thinking you were dead. Cazzo d'un cane! And you alive, and me a fool. (De Bernières, 1995, p. 518)

As it was with their first battle for dominance, Antonio manages to tame the wild and violent goddess by his wisdom, care, and love which reach the other side of Pelagia, that of a caregiver and a lover, a harmless and a caring consort. By explaining how often he has come to see her, how much he has cared and loved her all these years, and by revealing the truth of having dedicated his entire creative life to her, he succeeds in removing all Pelagia's fears and insecurities.

The union of opposites – masculine and feminine – is a characteristic metaphor for the individuation process. Jung names it as the "mysterium coniunctionis", symbolically represented by the conjunction of Sol and Luna, and signifying the completion of the alchemical opus.

The essential function of Corelli's and Pelagia's "marriage" refers to the union of all archetypes of the unconscious, when the power and wisdom confront the possible anxieties of the personal unconscious.

The wisdom of the hero and the heroine is implied in their effort to go beyond the interests of the ego while cultivating feelings of care and love for others, which is an effort leading them to the accomplishment of their integrated personalities. The security provided by the unconditional love of both characters and the capacity of each individual to share this love contribute to the psychological wholeness of the hero and the heroine.

Pelagia's and Antonio's union is revealed by their ride on the motorbike, defying time, obstacles, and prejudices. With all their strength and courage,

> they veered perilously along the stony roads, she clung to his waist, white-knuckled with terror, her face buried between his shoulder-blades, the machine thundering in her groin with a sensation that was at once deeply pleasant and thoroughly disturbing. Corelli noticed that she clutched him even more desperately than in the old days, and cynically he inserted some deliberate swerves into the series of those which were alarmingly accidental. (De Bernières, 1995, p. 532)

The union of the two lovers in this fragment brings to mind the conceit developed by John Donne in his famous poem *The Good-Morrow*: "Let sea-discoverers to new worlds have gone, / Let maps to other, worlds on worlds have shown, / Let us possess one world; each hath one, and is one". The conceit makes itself present in this stanza in the striking declaration that each lover is a world, but through love, the lovers create a single world of their own, that is to say, a world made up of the union of their souls.

Through this association, Pelagia and Antonio represent each an individual universe, but in their union, they manage to complete each other and to create one perfect world derived from the strength of their true feelings of love and compassion. This world symbolises their accomplishment of wholeness. Their fusion is strong and complete, and is free from extremes and any possibilities of decay.

In the same poem, Donne further claims that "whatever dies was not mixed equally", by which he draws on the alchemical notion of equally mixed substances that cannot disappear or change, and, if anything perishes, it is because the substance were imperfectly mixed. As in Donne's metaphysical poem, our two lovers, Antonio and Pelagia, enjoy a promised perpetual ecstasy that holds them together, neither of them falling away from exhaustion, but becoming immortal through their non-perishing love.

Through their union, they create an apotheosis of love, transcending the limits of time and revealing an enthusiasm of living together a new experience that both arrests and conquers the time. Their mutual excitement reveals their conjugal commitment and serves as a metaphor for their being alive and defeating the passage of time. The acceleration of the motorbike and the swerves created by Antonio represent their anticipation and frenzy of their future existence together as a new journey of two completed and above all united Selves.

Perhaps the best way to summarize the heroine's journey is to use Jean Bolen's words which stress the complexity and individuality of the quest: "The heroine's trip is a journey of discovery and development, of integrating aspects of herself into a whole, yet complex personality" (Bolen, 1984, p. 283).

Indeed, the accomplishment of a harmonious self crowned by the triumph over obstacles, such as prejudices, rejection, silencing, domination, frustration, and passage of time, represents the final victory of the heroine.

Conclusion

The paradigm of the monomyth of the hero and the quest as a journey of human soul has generated a great fascination on various writers and readers of all times, and it does not come as a surprise to discover that such a renowned author as Louis de Bernières has found it to be a great source of inspiration in his endeavours to represent human experience in the contemporary world.

The mythic journey of the hero as a psychic experience is revealed in *Captain Corelli's Mandolin* in terms of a fundamental experience of the individual living in an alien postmodern world. The framework of the monomyth provides the possibility of following the trajectory of the exterior journeys performed by the protagonists, but it is their interior journey that acquires a symbolical significance for the search of the self and the accomplishment of a true goal in life.

Louis de Bernières does not simply retell the monomyth. By the help of certain easily recognizable mythic situations, which are frequently subverted or inverted, the British writer finds an opportunity to rethink the monomyth, and revise the worth of public and private deeds in the contemporary community.

At the same time, Louis de Bernières' rethinking and rewriting of the monomyth incorporate a new stage. Contrary to Joseph Campbell's formula which implies that the hero's journey ends with his return home, de Bernières shows that the hero's and heroine's journey never ends, and that the end of a voyage implies the beginning of a new one, since the character's journey is cyclical and can be reiterated many times.

In the course of events, the hero's and heroine's system of values, including their moral ones, may collapse as a result of fear, aspiration to succeed, desire to hold power, or materialism.

The hero or heroine may forget or choose to ignore the earlier attained and assumed values and instructions, preferring instead to turn into a deceptive bigot, or an autocrat, or let the spirit be dominated by doubt and frustration. It is now that a new journey is necessary, when he or she must reconsider his or her true goal in life, detach from the bestial self and rediscover once again the humane side and, consequently, the self.

In conclusion, we are entitled to say that Louis de Bernières envisages a new pattern of the heroic quest, in which the major focus is no longer on conquest or domination. Instead, he presents a new heroic paradigm based on the union of opposites, and the integration and self-accomplishment through connection with others.

Contrary to the established pattern of the monomyth, Louis de Bernières' model does not present a dominant hero or heroine. His revised monomyth discloses a relationship based on interdependence in both private and public realms. Above all, de Bernières subverts Campbell's depiction of the hero who acts alone in his attempt to transform the community. The alternative presented by Louis de Bernières brings into attention two people – the hero and the heroine – who perform different deeds on personal and public levels in order to renew together their world.

The last thing to be mentioned in the conclusion is that Louis de Bernières creates his paradigm of the hero and heroine based on models of personal ethical conduct, at best defined by Sidney Hook:

> The paradigm of all occasions of genuine moral choice, whether private or public, is not the conflict between the good and the bad, the right and the wrong (…) but the conflict between the good and the good, the right and the right, and the good and the right. Whatever problems we analyse in private or public morality, we shall find that there is no one moral absolute except the moral obligation to choose intelligently, i.e., to choose that course of conduct whose consequences will strengthen the structure of the reflective values that define our philosophy of life. (Hook, 1978, pp. 7–8)

This is the only heroic attitude which is acceptable in the contemporary world after the witnessing of so many calamities and disasters produced in the course of history of humanity, the last of which being the atrocities and painful experiences of the Second World War.

The postmodern literature employs apocalyptic motifs and refuses to believe optimistically in success and accomplishment, but Louis de Bernières, in his *Captain Corelli's Mandolin*, even though uses similar disturbing and dislocating motifs, develops a happy-end and offers a hope.

References and Further Reading

Adams, Don (1997). *James Merrill's Poetic Quest*. Westport: Greenwood.
Aisenberg, Nadya (1994). *Ordinary Heroines: Transforming the Male Myth*. New York: Continuum.
Aurobindo, Sri (1996). *Letters on Yoga*. Pondicherry: Sri Aurobindo Ashram.
Barthes, Roland (1991). *Mythologies*. New York: The Noonday Press.
Bell, Michael (1997). *Literature, Modernism and Myth*. Cambridge: Cambridge University Press.
Betsch, Tilmann (2008). The Nature of Intuition and Its Neglect in Research on Judgment and Decision-Making. In Henning Plessner, Cornelia Betsch, Tilmann Betsch (Eds.), *Intuition in Judgment and Decision-Making*. New York: Taylor & Francis.
Bolen, Jean Shinoda (1984). *Goddesses in Everywoman: Powerful Archetypes in Women's Lives*. New York: Harper Perrenial.
Bolen, Jean Shinoda (1989). *Gods in Everyman: A New Psychology of Men's Lives and Loves*. San Francisco: Harper and Row.
Brunel, Pierre (1992). *Companion to Literary Myths, Heroes and Archetypes*. London: Routledge.
Campbell, Joseph (1968). *The Hero with a Thousand Faces*. Princeton: Princeton University Press.
Campbell, Joseph (1988). *The Power of Myth, with Bill Moyers*. New York: Doubleday.
Covington, Coline (July 1989). In Search of the Heroine. In *The Journal of Analytical Psychology*, Volume 34, Issue 3, pages 243–254. London: The Society of Analytical Psychology.
Crone, Anna Lisa (2010). *Eros and Creativity in Russian Religious Renewal: The Philosophers and the Freudians*. Boston: Brill Academic Publishers.
Dalai Lama (15 March, 2010). *Compassion and the Individual*, Messages.
Dardell, Eric (1984). The Mythic. In Alan Dundes (Ed.), *Sacred Narrative: Readings in the Theory of Myth*. Berkeley: University of California Press.
De Bernières, Louis (1995). *Captain Corelli's Mandolin*. London: Vintage Books.
Dubuisson, Daniel (2006). *Twentieth Century Mythologies: Dumézil, Lévi-Strauss, Eliade*. London: Equinox Publishing.
Durand, G. (1998). *Figuri mitice şi chipuri ale operei: De la mitocritică la mitanaliză*. Bucureşti: Nemira.

Eisler, Riane (1997). Introduction. In Carolyne Larrington (Ed.), *The Woman's Companion to Mythology*. London: Pandora.
Eliade, Mircea (1963). *Myth and Reality*. New York: Harper and Row.
Erikson, Erik (1975). *Life, History and the Historical Moment*. New York: W. W. Norton and Co.
Estés, Clarissa Pinkola (1992). *Women Who Run with the Wolves*. New York: Ballantine.
Freiberg, L. (1965). New views of art and the creative process in psychoanalytical ego psychology. In H. Ruitenbeek (Ed.), *The Creative Imagination*. Chicago: Quadrangle Books.
Freidenberg, Olga (1997). *Image and Concept: Mythopoetic Roots of Literature*. Amsterdam: Harwood Academic Publishers.
Freud, Sigmund ([1901], 1953–1966). The Psychopathology of Everyday Life. In James Strachey (Ed.), *The Standard Edition of the Complete Psychological Works of Sigmund Freud* (vol. 6). London: The Hogarth Press.
Fromm, Erich (1973). *The Anatomy of Human Destructiveness*. New York: Holt, Rinehart and Winston.
Guillen, Claudio (1993). *The Challenge of Comparative Literature*. Cambridge: Harvard University Press.
Gurian, Michael (1994). *Mothers, Sons & Lovers: How a Man's Relationship with His Mother Affects the Rest of His Life*. London: Shambhala.
Hagman, George (2005). *Contemporary Psychoanalytic Studies, Volume 5: Aesthetic Experience: Beauty, Creativity, and the Search for the Ideal*. Amsterdam: Editions Rodopi.
Henderson, Joseph (1964). Ancient Myths and Modern Man. In Carl Jung (Ed.), *Man and His Symbols*. Garden City: Doubleday.
Hook, Sidney (1978). *The Hero in History: Myth, Power, or Moral Ideal?*. Stanford: Stanford University.
Jacobi, Jolande (1951). *The Psychology of C. G. Jung*. New Haven: Yale University Press.
Jung, Carl ([1959], 1969). The Archetypes and the Collective Unconscious. In Gerhard Adler and R. F. C. Hull (Eds.), *The Collected Works of C. G. Jung* (vol. 9). London: Routledge and Kegan Paul.
Jung, Carl (1963). *Memories, Dreams, Reflections*. New York: Pantheon Books.
Jung, Carl (1971). Aion: Phenomenology of the Self. In Joseph Campbell (Ed.), *The Portable Jung*. New York: Viking Press.
Jung, Carl (1983). *The Essential Jung: Selected Writings*. London: Fontana.

Keen, Sam (1986). *Faces of the Enemy: Reflections of the Hostile Imagination*. San Francisco: HarperCollins Publishers.
Kimmel, Michael (2000). *The Gendered Society*. Oxford: Oxford University Press.
Knapp, Bettina L. (1997). *Women in Myth*. Albany: SUNY Press.
Kushner, E. (2001). *Living Prism: Itineraries in Comparative Literature*. Montreal: McGill-Queen's University Press.
Laing, R. D. (1979). *The Divided Self*. New York: Penguin Books.
Leeming, David Adams (1990). *The World of Myth*. Oxford: Oxford University Press.
Leeming, David Adams (2001). *Myth: A Biography of Belief*. Oxford: Oxford University Press.
Lévi-Strauss, Claude (1990). *The Naked Man, Mythologiques Volume Four*. Chicago: University of Chicago Press.
Lowry, Shirley Park (1982). *Familiar Mysteries: The Truth in Myth*. Oxford: Oxford University Press.
Lyotard, Jean-François (1989). *The Lyotard Reader* (ed. Andrew Benjamin). Oxford: Blackwell.
Meade, Michael (October 2009). *Stories for the End Times, Lecture*. Port Townsend: Quimper Unitarian Universalist Church.
Murdock, Maureen (1990). *The Heroine's Journey: Woman's Quest for Wholeness*. Boston: Shambhala Publications.
Murdock, Maureen (2005). *Fathers' Daughters: Breaking the Ties that Bind*. New Orleans: Spring.
Noel, Daniel C. (1991). Revisioning the Hero. In Christine Downing (Ed.), *Mirrors of the Self: Archetypal Images that Shape Your Life*. Los Angeles: Jeremy P. Tarcher.
Pearson, Carol S., and Pope, Katherine (1981). *The Female Hero in American and British Literature*. New York: R. R. Bowker Company.
Pearson, Carol S. (1989). *The Hero Within: Six Archetypes We Live By*. New York: Harper and Row.
Pearson, Carol S. (1991). *Awakening the Heroes Within: Twelve Archetypes to Help Us Find Ourselves and Transform Our World*. New York: Harper Collins Publishers.
Pipher, Mary (1994). *Reviving Ophelia: Saving the Selves of Adolescent Girls*. New York: Ballantine.
Powers, Meredith A. (1991). *The Heroine in Western Literature: The Archetype and Her Reemergence in Modern Prose*. Jefferson: McFarland.

Pratt, Annis (1981). *Archetypal Patterns in Women's Fiction*. Bloomington: Indiana University Press.
Raymond, Janice G. (2001). *A Passion for Friends: Toward a Philosophy of Female Affection*. North Melbourne: Spinifex.
Redfield, James (1997). *The Celestine Vision: Living the New Spiritual Awareness*. New York: Warner Books.
Rochelle, Warren G. (2000). *Communities of the Heart: The Rhetoric of Myth in the Fiction of Ursula K. Le Guin*. Liverpool: Liverpool University Press.
Rose, Gilbert J. (1992). *The Power of Form: A Psychoanalytic Approach to Aesthetic Form*. New York: International Universities Press.
Rosen, Charles (2003). *Piano Notes*. London: Allen Lane.
Schierse Leonard, Linda (1982). *The Wounded Woman: Healing the Father-Daughter Relationship*. Boston: Shambhala Publications.
Segal, Robert A. (1987). *Joseph Campbell: An Introduction*. New York: Garland.
Sharpe, R. A. (2004). *Philosophy of Music*. Durham: Acumen.
Stone, R. G. (1967). Myth in Modern French Literature. In Margaret Dalziel (Ed.), *Myth and the Modern Imagination*. Dunedin: University of Otaga Press.
Walker, Steven F. (1992). *Jung and the Jungians on Myth*. New York: Garland.
White, John J. (1971). *Mythology in the Modern Novel: A Study of Prefigurative Techniques*. Princeton: Princeton University Press.

Index

A
Adams, Don 65, 115
Aisenberg, Nadya 115
Aurobindo, Sri 64, 115

B
Barthes, Roland 26, 115
Bell, Michael 13, 62, 115
Betsch, Tilmann 100, 115
Bolen, Jean Shinoda 115
Brunel, Pierre 33, 115

C
Campbell, Joseph 8, 20, 115
Camus, Albert 100
Covington, Coline 81, 115
Crone, Anna Lisa 115

D
Dalai Lama 64, 115
Dante 53, 58
Dardell, Eric 115
De Bernières, Louis 7–114
De Saussure, Ferdinand 27
Donne, John 111
Dubuisson, Daniel 24, 115
Durand, Gilbert 14, 15, 115

E
Eisler, Riane 116
Eliade, Mircea 14, 116
Eliot, T. S. 14
Erikson, Erik 116
Estés, Clarissa Pinkola 87, 92, 99, 102, 108, 116

F
Frazer, J. G. 19
Freiberg, Louis 67, 116

Freidenberg, Olga 15, 116
Freud, Sigmund 14, 38, 116
Fromm, Erich 55, 116
Frye, Northrop 14

G
Guillen, Claudio 14, 116
Gurian, Michael 49, 116

H
Hagman, George 66, 73, 116
Henderson, Joseph 34, 116
Homer 32, 35
Hook, Sidney 114, 116

J
Jacobi, Jolande 116
Jolles, Andre 14
Joyce, James 22, 33
Jung, Carl 8, 15, 20, 116

K
Keen, Sam 117
Kimmel, Michael 43, 117
Knapp, Bettina L. 97, 117
Kris, Ernst 68
Kushner, E. 117

L
Laing, R. D. 49, 117
Leeming, David Adams 13, 117
Lévi-Strauss, Claude 8, 117
Lowry, Shirley Park 117
Lyotard, Jean-François 14, 117

M
Meade, Michael 97, 117
Murdock, Maureen 79, 86, 88, 92, 94, 95, 97, 103, 106, 109, 117

N
Neumann, Erich 34
Nietzsche, Friedrich Wilhelm 62
Noel, Daniel C. 117

O
Ovid 32

P
Pearson, Carol S. 92, 117
Pipher, Mary 117
Powers, Meredith A. 117
Pratt, Annis 104, 114, 118

R
Raymond, Janice G. 91, 118
Redfield, James 38, 58, 118
Rochelle, Warren G. 118

Rose, Gilbert J. 68–70, 118
Rosen, Charles 70, 118

S
Schierse Leonard, Linda 88, 118
Schopenhauer, Arthur 16
Segal, Robert A. 118
Sharpe, R. A. 67, 70, 118
Stone, R. G. 13, 118

V
Virgil 32

W
Wagner, Wilhelm Richard 62, 63
Walker, Steven F. 118
White, John J. 13, 118

www.ingramcontent.com/pod-product-compliance
Ingram Content Group UK Ltd.
Pitfield, Milton Keynes, MK11 3LW, UK
UKHW021836210426
5322IPUK00021B/327